Omega-3 Protein Diet

David Galsworthy

Published by
Lignan Nutritional Publications

Omega-3 Protein Diet

David A Galsworthy

Copyright © David Galsworthy, 2001

The moral right of the author has been asserted
All rights reserved. Without limiting the rights under copyright reserved above, no part of this publication may be reproduced, stored in or introduced into a retrieval system, or transmitted, in any form or by any means (electronic, mechanical, photocopying, recording or other wise), without the prior written permission of both the copyright owner and the above publisher of this book.

Printed and bound in Great Britain

The Author

David Galsworthy was born in London in 1948 and raised in the Essex suburbs. I have known and worked with David for more than 20 years and the shock with what was to follow for such a fit and healthy friend did not bode well. In April 1999 David returned from an overseas business trip with what was believed to be food poisoning. Treatment began with anti-biotic medication for a bladder infection, but the underlying condition did not clear up and in fact began to get worse until he was passing large amounts of blood in the urine. In August of the same year the bladder infection was diagnosed as advanced prostate cancer with secondary metastasis to the liver, kidney and bone, and he was given only 'several months' to survive. Embarking on what can only be described as a steep learning curve of the immune system, nutrition, the human body responses and confidence in his own ability to discover a way to beat such a debilitating illness he began to nourish his body with natural foods, removing all processed and refined food from his diet. His quality of life began to improve considerably but from the regular monthly conventional blood tests and unconventional humoral blood tests it was apparent that the illness was lying dormant waiting to strike at any time. Many old colleagues wanted to help, but as onlookers we are powerless except to give as much encouragement as we can. In November 1999 a dozen or so of David's past colleagues and friends from all over the world met in London for a 'one-off' reunion dinner which was at the same time a surprise for David. We all thought it would be his last. In September 2000 the existing conventional medication began to fail and the future really did look bleak. David was referred to Professor Tim Oliver, Medical Director of Oncology at St. Bartholomew's Hospital. The prognosis again was not good. David was informed that he had a 1 in 20 chance of surviving about 6 months, and there was little chance of reversing the liver and bone metastasis. A combination of drugs including some pretty nasty chemotherapy was administered. Some weeks prior to the chemotherapy, David had begun the Omega-3 Protein Diet, he noted in his diary that he had begun to feel better with improved energy levels, skin improvement and an unexplained calmness. David suffered none of the associated side effects of the chemotherapy and life continued as if nothing was wrong. Most friends could not believe how well he looked throughout the chemotherapy regime. We are even thinking of arranging another one-off reunion bash, the wine had flowed so well.

The culmination of David's work was in April 2001 when Professor Oliver, his oncologist informed him that the cancer may have gone. The CT scans and blood results all indicated an apparent disappearance of tumours, the liver metastasis, one of which was 3.75cm in diameter had vanished. The results of 'the road to recovery' and diet follow in this book. It details the Omega-3 Protein Diet programme that David designed and used along with the wholesome food recipes that will benefit not only the chronically ill but also any one who just wants to stay healthy and fit.

As a result of David's "remarkable" recovery (Quote Consultant Surgeon Mr. James Hill) almost all of his family, relatives, friends and acquaintances are now using varying levels of the diet in one form or another and noticing marked improvement in their health and well being. *McCleod*

Flaxseed Oil and Flaxseed Flake form an important part of the Omega-3 Protein Diet as does some simple nutrition recipes. The constituent parts of Flaxseed, primarily 'The Omega Oils' work at the cellular level within the body repairing metabolic processes that have either been damaged or are failing. Omega-3 is extensively researched, and is better known in the UK as a fatty acid associated with Cod Liver Oil.

However, with the known and proven health benefits to a number of illnesses or ailments this book does not suggest that Flaxseed is the panacea for all of our ills. **Never The Less, Research May Prove It Very Soon!**

It is strongly recommended that any individual who is suffering with an illness should consult their professional medical carer or doctor before embarking on any significant dietary changes.

The *Omega 3-Protein Diet* and the contents of this book are meant to inform and educate with regards to nutritional assistance. Recommendations herein are not to be taken as a therapeutic treatment for any particular illness or cure for any ailment or medical condition.

To C, Always With Me - For Her Love & Support

ACKNOWLEDGEMENTS

To Lauren and Jay for their love and
tolerance of an occasional manic father
Jan and Sylvie, Val and Glynn - all very dear friends
To Peter, Big Bad John, Alistair and Nev for keeping me smiling

For giving me back my life I would like to thank
Professor Tim Oliver MD, F.R.C.P.
Mr James T. Hill MB, F.R.C.S.
Dr Jay Jain,
Professor David Schweitzer
Dr Marc Mortiboys

The A&E night crew at Oldchurch Hospital led by Kathy
on my three unexpected visits.
Oliver's Angels: Carmel, Uma and Esther

Professor Lillian Thompson, University Of Toronto
Professor Michael Hyland – Plymouth University
Dr Jon Davies
Sally Fallon – Weston A Price Foundation
Dr Joseph Mercola / www.mercola.com

Dr Johanna Budwig who picked up the pieces and
gave medical science something to think about

Chris Cumbers for putting me on the right track with ACV.

And, not forgetting 'My Inspiration'

Other works available by the same author
**Do You Know What Your Eating
(A thousand foods analysed)**
Expected publication date: February 2002

INTRODUCTION	9
Are We Really The Civilised Ones!	11
A Marriage In Heaven	22
Picking Up The Pieces	24
What The Doctor's, Experts & Media Say!	29
Getting To Know Flax Seed	31
Inside Flaxseed – What You Will Find	33
What Is Flax Seed	41
Sourcing, Preparing and Storing Flax Seed	46
What Do I Need To Take?	48
How To Take Flaxseed Oil	50
Rules For A Healthy Body	51
Discovering Your Daily Protein Intake	51
Ideal Body Weight Charts:	53
Why Our Body's Need Fat!	58
Other Beneficial Fatty Acid Oils	59
When Your Told It's Cancer	64
Nutrition and Cancer Conference	67
CT Scans The Author's Liver	69
The Body's Cleansing Organs	72
Mad As A Hatter - Is Dental Amalgam Safe?	75
Cancer of the Large Bowel (Colon and Rectum)	77
Bowel Cancer Surgery	79
Breast Cancer - Prevented Naturally!	82
Omega-3-Protein Diet - V For Victory Not Victim	87
Menopause and PMS - Is This Nature's Answer?	91
Who's In Charge of Your Change	92
Omega-3-Protein Diet - Let Your Diet Take The Strain	95
The 3P's - Preventing Prostate Problems	99
Omega-3 Protein Diet - An Aid For Prostate Problems	101
Loose That Fat - Eat More Fat!	105
Omega-3 Protein Diet - An Aid To Weight Loss	109

Arthritis – Flax Seed A Potential Aid 114
   Omega-3 Protein Diet - An Aid For Arthritis 118
Lowering Cholesterol And Blood Pressure 123
   Omega-3 Protein Diet - An Aid To Reducing Blood Pressure 127
Preventing Heart Attacks & Strokes 131
   How about those individuals who already have heart disease? 135
Stroke – A Preventable Malady 136
   Omega-3 Protein Diet - An Aid To Preventing Heart Infarction and Stroke 143
Preventing Osteoporosis 147
   Omega-3 Protein Diet - An Aid For Osteoporosis 151
Diabetes 155
   Omega-3 Protein Diet - For The Diabetic 164
Explaining – The Omega-3 Protein Diet 168
Athletes, Sports Person Or Simply Energetic! 172
   Omega-3 Protein Diet® - Athletically Fit and Well 175
Pregnancy and Omega 3 178
Breakfast For The Young 180
Stock Making 181
Stock, Broth And Soup Making 185
Food & Kitchen Basics 192
   Is Organic Best? 196
   What Oil Is Best For Cooking 200
The Super Health Foods 201
Recipes – Grand Ma Knew Best 208
Flax seed Breads & Pastries 209
Vegetarian Dishes 212
Vegetable Dishes 212
Meat Dishes 224
Organic Meat Suppliers 248
Therapeutic Recipes 250
Sources 251
Health Care Associations 252

8

INTRODUCTION

The incidence of people suffering with chronic health conditions has been increasing year on year over the last century. An example is that in the early 1900's the possibilities of someone contracting a cancer related illness had an approximate 3% chance, now that has risen to something more than 25% and some experts are even reporting a 33% risk. Heart infarction, stroke, diabetes and many other degenerative illnesses or diseases have increased significantly also. Heart disease is now the biggest killer in the United States as well as many other countries, and it need not be. The Journal of Clinical Nutrition publishing it's finding on diabetes indicating that the illness had reached 'epidemic' proportions and the increase last year (2000) in the 30-year old age group was up by 70%.

Conventional medicine has tried to keep pace, without much success. New treatments, new drugs and new research come and go – one treatment replaces another. Ground breaking ideas and research can take 10 or more years to get to the patient. In the meantime people suffering with chronic illness have to make do with what conventional pharmaceutical drugs have to offer. Very few offer a cure, most only a treatment option for the symptoms. The cure is in the hands of your own body. The most potent weapon we possess for fighting and eventually curing an illness is within our own immune system.

The cause of many chronic illnesses can be identified by two important factors:
- Inadequate and Unbalanced Nutrition – Leading to failure of the body to metabolise vital body functions and degradation of the immune system.
- Toxic Inhibiting Elements from Food and the Environment – Leading to inhibition of the immune systems response.

With the pressures and stresses of modern working and living our bodies need more relaxation and greater nutrition. Nutritional food products are all around us, imports from the other-side of the world, exotic vegetables and fruit much of which were unheard of only 50 years ago.

The simplicity now-days of pre-cooked dinners or suppers, take away meals; all of these help us live a faster convenient life style. But, do we really know what we are eating, do we really know what nutrition we are putting inside our body's every day?

If you don't, then you had better carry on reading!

Just think a moment of this analogy: Your driving down the motorway, maybe you have your partner with you or the kids in the back and you may even be lucky enough to be getting a few days away from the rigours of work. The oil light begins to flash on the dashboard. Lucky for you a service station is only one mile ahead. What do you do – obvious really, you pull in and top up the engine with oil, and you can carry on your merry way?

But what happens if there is not a service station a mile down the road or you think to yourself 'I've only got 20 mile to my destination I'll top it up there'. If your lucky you may get away with it, if not you may have cost yourself a thousand or two for a replacement engine, ruined your trip and had the other half nagging you for being so stupid.

Well imagine your body as the car and your immune system as the engine. Just like your car engine your immune system needs regular maintenance and you can service it every day with a balanced nutritional diet, or supplement it with vitamins and minerals if necessary just as you did on the motorway by calling in for a top up of oil.

Unfortunately with our body's engine we cannot go and spend a thousand or two if it all goes wrong, we rarely have anything to replace it with.

Our body's immune system is an extremely complex system, which even as we start the 21st Century cannot be fully explained. Scientists, biochemists and nutritional experts specialising in the human immune system often know the results of certain chemical reactions in the body but cannot always explain why some of them occur.

Are We Really The Civilised Ones!

For decades the diet plan discussed in this small piece of work has proven to have preventative and therapeutic benefits for many if not most chronic illnesses. Until recently conventional medicine and many doctors have dismissed the association and benefits of good nutrition in combating serious debilitating illnesses, many of which may be reversed with a good healthy balanced diet without the need of toxic pharmaceutical medications. As will be discussed later many of the illnesses afflicting our civilised society are growing at such an alarming rate that to describe the situation as an 'epidemic' would not necessarily be an over statement. Unless our modern society grasps the problems and unfortunately we cannot leave it to those charged with looking after our health, we will decline into poor specimens, not what Mother Nature intended. We need to make those changes ourselves in our nutrition, fitness and awareness of what foods are good and what foods are bad for us.

Fortunately in the last decade or so there has been an increase in our societies awareness of food issues – it seems all of us have woken up. Gymnasiums are now common-place, health food stores have immerged to give us the benefit of supplements and the supermarkets are now increasing their range of organic food products. None of these would have come about if it were not for societies acceptance and the demand for new health ideas and nutritious produce. With the introduction of organic foods it gives some encouragement to know that we may at last be back on track to nourishing our body's correctly – or are we?

Gymnasiums allow us to exercise, an important requirement for a healthy body. Health food stores have blossomed due to public demand – some individuals have realised at last that our foods are so heavily processed we need to supplement them on a regular basis – or could it be that many more individuals are seeking complimentary and alternative therapies for their ailments.

Understanding that we need to consume healthy foods is paramount in staying fit and well and allowing our bodies to thrive and overcome illness. We need to consume foods that will renew, regenerate and optimise our immune response and our metabolic respiration (renewal of cells). Eating healthy, nutritious foods has been proven to reduce the incidence of chronic illness by almost 50% - is that not encouraging!

How Our Eating Patterns Evolved
In days gone by our distant ancestors were most probably healthier than we are today. Long before our industrialised society, our predecessor's foods came mostly from the land in the form of fruits, vegetables, seeds and nuts – then it was balanced intentionally with meat, dairy produce and some cereals and whole grains. Sugar, natural of course was available from root crops, fruits and berries. Milled flours were processed as whole grains and the flesh from the meat they ate in their diet was abundantly nutritious from the pasture fed cattle or wild animal stock.
But in today's hectic world almost all of these 'natural' nutritious foods are difficult (not impossible) to find. The diet in our modern society has changed dramatically for the worse and we now consume foods that are calorifically abundant but devoid of adequate nutrition. Our diet is now predominantly from animal and dairy produce whilst the valuable vegetable plant type food and whole grain cereals take a back seat.
Processed, convenient, fast, pre-cooked this pre-packaged that – these foods are often too high in the incorrect fats, refined sugars and protein. Now…by the time the food processors - food processors is the wrong job description for them - we'll think of another by the end of the book! – decide to pollute the already nutritionally devoid product with preservatives, colouring, stabilizers, E's and whatever….and they still have the neck to call it food.
Sorry chaps back to school – or is it the chemistry lab!
Diverging for a moment, the dictionary definition for food is: (f__d) *n.* matter which one feeds on; that, which is absorbed by any organism, promotes growth; solid nourishment as contrary with liquids.
Are we really sure what we eat should be described as food?

12

As you will read later we need to balance our foods, especially fats (the good one), proteins need to be moderated and carbohydrates identified for those that are good for our bodies.

And We Call Them Primitive!

Eskimos, Hunzas, Georgians are just a few of the many groups of indigenous people around the world whose diet do not include processed or refined foods. Almost all members of these groups of people enjoy excellent health, many living to be centarians who are almost free of cancer, heart infarction and many of the other degenerative diseases afflicting our so-called civilised informed society.

All of these groups follow a diet that is natural and nutritious. The Hunzas diet is rich in minerals, complete proteins from millet, soy-beans, barley, buckwheat as well as natural foods of almonds, sesame seed, green leaf vegetables, fruit, berries and a variety of sprouted seeds. The Mediterranean's have a diet that includes, olive oil, garlic, onions, tomatoes and grapes – mostly natural, unrefined and fresh but all abundant in antioxidants, with a wealth of nutrients. The Eskimo's whose diet is exceptionally high in saturated fat have an extremely low incidence of heart or cardiovascular problems almost zero cancer related illnesses – and they tell us that fat is the cause of heart disease and cancer – maybe it is another fat.

Now…. This is where it gets really interesting….!

They Stand Indicted

Dr Johanna Budwig, Professor Lillian Thompson, Drs. Udo Erasmus, John McDougall, Neil Barnard, Professor Mary Enig may not have realised initially the significance of their individual and invaluable work in the early days of their research, but putting it mildly these eminent forward thinking doctors, scientists and researchers may well have begun to save the average individual from debilitating illnesses or premature mortality.

All of them have recognised that our health over the past 100 years has declined to such an extent that most individuals body's may only be functioning at 60% of its potential and that is if we believe we are feeling well. Imagine if our bodies were functioning at near optimum performance of healthfulness, the result, a lower incidence of common ailments, illness and an improved quality of life through to old age, with plenty of enjoyable mad moments to look back to.

Our modern civilised society has become one that is more concerned with image consciousness, youthfulness and unhealthy methods of weight consciousness, than the necessary natural nutrition of our body's. Weight is a very important factor for staying healthy, obesity is a killer, but it is the way individuals go about the weight reduction that gives the greatest concern *(see chapter on weight)*.

Our diet and the food western society now consumes compared to that prior to around 1910 has gradually become deficient in some of the most vital nutrients known to man and those nutrients are desperately needed so that our body's can function properly every day. Whilst our foods have almost become 'non foods', we have also been ingesting at the same time some extremely bad fats and oils that have literally been poisoning us for almost 90 years.

Cardiovascular Disease (CVD) has increased to an alarming level, coronary occlusion was first medically recorded in 1910. Cardiovascular disease 90 years ago from all causes amounted to only 15% of the population, now that figure has increased by more than 300% to a figure today of 45% of a supposedly more informed society.

Cancer related mortality accounted for less than 3% of the population 100 years ago – today cancer related illnesses kills 30% of the populace and afflicts more than 40% which is up from 1 in 10 in the last 10 years and it is still rising at an alarming rate.

Sixty or so years ago diabetes afflicted only 1 in 100,000 people – today 1 in 12 of the population are receiving treatment for either type I or type II diabetes and again the incidence of diagnosed diabetes is rising more dramatically than any other illness, as I mentioned earlier, last year - 30 year old individuals becoming afflicted with diabetes increased by 70% in one year alone!

The fourth leading cause of death is Alzheimer's Disease – 100 years ago there were NO recorded cases of this most debilitating age related illness and there is doubt whether it actually existed in those times.

Other degenerative illnesses such as MS, Kidney or Liver malfunctions and Osteoporosis have increased at such an alarming rate within the past couple of decades the medical profession have no way of keeping up with the treatment.

Obesity is another problem, much more serious than most individuals realise. It is currently affecting 50% of most Western Societies and even more alarming 35% of children below the age of 5 years are 'officially' classed as obese.

How have we allowed our body's to become so inefficient at preventing chronic illness, inbound toxins and infection. Why have has society allowed obesity to take control of our body's. Read on because there is most certainly a likely culprit and we welcome it with open arms every day, unwittingly.

We Have Been Hoodwinked, Misinformed and Lied To.

Why with all the apparent improvements in medical science are doctors unable to keep up with the ever increasing toll of chronic illness? Why are illnesses running out of control. We may be living longer, but is the quality of life available.

How many people do you know at 65 years of age or even 55 years who are completely free of arthritis, not many I bet!

A little of the blame is with ourselves for the fashionable life style we lead although with the media marketing for some unhealthy food products much of the blame has to pass to those -

'Who Stand Indicted'.

With this current malaise anyone would think it was an alien invasion that has caused our body's to become debilitated. Sorry to disappoint you but it is much closer to home I am afraid!

We are poisoning ourselves unintentionally.

Our body's homeostasis, which is the metabolic, biochemical process and immune system response and functioning has been disrupted by one likely culprit, one that we greet with great pleasure several times a day.

The diet ridden culture for no-fat/low-fat and its proponents have much to answer for; the four letter words oils or fats send them cowering to a corner. It is extremely rare for the fat conscious individual to even consider entertaining any fat or oil within their diet. But some fats or more specifically oils have the most positive benefit to our body and metabolic system and without several of them we could not survive. These are not only essential they are vital for a well-oiled body, a body that can thrive and fight off infection and illness.

Obesity in our population and most alarmingly among children is at epidemic proportions and the figure of 'official' obesity is running too high - but by simply eliminating the truly bad fats and oils in our diet the incidence of obesity could either be totally eradicated from our society or at least reduced to a level that can be dealt with.

During the last decade a growing number of well informed doctors and scientists have highlighted the errors in our Western Society diet for the use of 'pseudo' fats and oils. Leading scientists many years ago pointed the finger at certain bad fats for the alarming rise in a variety of degenerative diseases, but they were not taken seriously and were thus described as cranks or loonies by those commercially interested parties –
The Food Oil Industry.

The Good, The Bad and The Poisonous.

Many nutritional writers put fats and oils into two categories and describe them as good fats and bad fats. Sorry lads and lassies there is another group 'The Poisonous':

The Good are those that give us nutrition and allow our body's to thrive. These are unrefined fats and oils but essentially the EFA's (Omega-3).

The Bad are some (not all) of the saturated fats (mostly animal and dairy) that we need within our diet, but these must be consumed in moderation as too much ingestion of them can cause obesity, diabetes, heart infarction or even cancer.

The Poisonous are the 'Hydrogenated Oils', 'Partially Hydrogenated Oils' and Trans Fatty Acids along with some refined oils that literally languish in our body's and induce tissue damage organ malfunction or putting it bluntly - poison us.

These 'pseudo' oils and fats cause untold damage and are a major factor to arthritis, diabetes, obesity, heart infarction, stroke and cancer leading eventually to premature mortality. These 'altered' or 'pseudo' oils and fats are frequently found in margarines, bakery items, spreads, shortenings, refined oils and canned/packaged processed foods. You will have to read the labels to ensure you are not about to ingest one of these nasty substances.

Before you start with 'This Guys Gone Crazy' – Why would many countries including the UK ask for the manufacturers and processors to voluntary reduce the levels of hydrogenated oils and trans fatty acids in our food products if there was not a health issue at stake – are those who are charged with looking after our health beginning to wake up to the epidemic and the damaging effect of these pseudo processed oils. Lets hope so!

Let us first look at the different types of fats.
Saturated fat: Mostly found in animal tissue and some vegetable and these are naturally saturated with hydrogen molecules and generally have a longer shelf life than the unsaturated variety. Most are solid at room and body temperature. However, butter, which is a saturated fat, is not solid at body temperature.
Unsaturated fat: Mostly from vegetables products, these oils do not have so many hydrogen molecules and are thus liquid at room temperature. Mother nature unfortunately never finished with just two oils and fats she subdivided the unsaturated fats into monounsaturated and polyunsaturated:

Mono and Poly unsaturated fat: These are safe oils so long as they are part of the originating grain and vegetable. However, when most of these oils are refined and separated from their originating source (grain or vegetable) and used as oils and fats in the commercial food industry, (cooking oils, margarines etc) they begin to have an extremely detrimental effect to our bodies if they have not been stored properly. In other words when processing of oil begin so do our health problems.

What do they do?
Some food manufacturers alter (process) polyunsaturated oils into something 'unnaturally' similar to saturated fat by the addition of more hydrogen atoms to the fat molecules, and we end up with hydrogenated oils and trans fatty acids, this is how they turn corn oil into margarine. All of this processing would not be so bad if the processed oils were good for us or had some nutritional value, but they are not, these altered oils are what are referred to as 'pseudo' oils or fats and they are extremely bad for our body's.

The alteration of oils for the food processing industry can be done in many different ways, bleaching, deodorising, heat treatment, hexane bathing all of which cause irreversible damage to the oil and then it is sold to us as food.

Sorry chaps you need to look up the dictionary meaning for the word 'food'.

Now can you understand why the fickle finger of fate has been pointed to the oil industry for some of our modern day health issues, and they are getting a little fidgety in the dock, because a number of very well informed scientists and doctors are grabbing public attention as to this intentional conspiracy.

The standing joke amongst nutritionists puts the altered oils and fats into prospective: 'they say that it is probably more healthy to eat the cardboard carton the margarine arrives in than it is to eat the margarine itself', animals and insects will not eat it so why should we.

Forming part of the unsaturated oils are the polyunsaturated oils and amongst these are several that are essential. Essential, in as much our bodies cannot synthesize them from any other food source and we need to ingest them directly ourselves from a food source rich in omega-3.

They are referred to as Essential Fatty Acids (EFA's) or Omega-3 is one, and Omega-6 is another.

These are the oils that I used to rid my body of cancer.

What did I do:
- Removed hydrogenated oils/TFAs and processed food from my diet
- Combined Omega 3 (Flaxseed oil) with Quark (protein).

That's all I did. Simple - You bet.

What I used and accomplished by reversing my illness may not work for everyone, as there are so many different modern day illnesses around caused by a myriad of modern day issues. But one thing is for sure if you follow just the basic diet programme you will begin to optimise your immune system and that is the most powerful, potent weapon you possess in combating illness.

Using flaxseed oil and flaxseed, Mother Nature's highest form of Omega-3, combined with removing the bad and 'non-foods' from your diet you'll begin to feel better and have less side effects from chemotherapy or pharmaceutical medications. Or if you're a diabetic your sugar levels will begin to normalise and for those cardiovascular problems you'll find some beneficial health enhancing factors.

Many of my family and friends are now using flax seed oil and flaxseed for just staying healthy or minor ailments, all of them are reporting significant improvement with their minor complaints.

How Did It All Happen?
The changes at the beginning of the last century came about not because of a population that were underfed but due to the 'Bigger Is Better' ideology of the food oil industry. The days of our mothers receiving fresh deliveries of some foods or the availability in the corner store of daily pressed oils have gone. The whole way in which large stores and supermarkets have to receive some of their produce is not ideal for storing fragile oils, so it was much easier for them to take what the food oil industry supplied. The consuming public were hoodwinked by the large oil processors many decades ago with the 'Butter Is Bad' – but 'Margarine Is Good' – science has now turned those contemptible remarks on there head. Butter is good for us in moderation, but processed margarine with hydrogenated oils and trans fatty acids (TFAs) is disastrous for us in any quantity.

By the 1920's the bigger is best theory had taken such a foot hold that the oil industry with massive processing factories were churning out thousands of tons of lifeless, inert oils for the consumers 24 hours a day. The product was more useful for greasing the axle bearings of a Model T Ford than ingestion by humans. The small, often family run oil producer and mill had little chance of surviving, some held on, most elbowed out, and by the time the Second World War started they had all but disappeared. Clever, deceptive advertising had sucked in the unwary and with the arrival of the 1950's, any sign of good nutritious oils were all but gone. Mums and Grand Mothers now had to use other methods of getting some decent nutrition or should I say Omega –3 inside their kids. As flaxseed was much more difficult to obtain they turned to the foul tasting cod liver oil for a nutritious supplement.

Our reverence for good tasting, nourishing food has now passed many decades ago. Packaged – TV Dinners – Micro Waved – Boil In The Bag food litter the supermarket shelves, we followed our North American cousins for convenient hydrogenated food stuff with greater enthusiasm than those in mainland Europe. They held fast and still hold many of their cooking traditions in great esteem, but the incidence of chronic illness gradually caught up with them too, as the march of the hydrogenated foods began to become more convenient and more popular with the younger generation. In the space of 30 years the 'big boys' of the food industry had turned our diet around from one that was nutritious to one that was deficient. It has been said that if the oil industry applied to those charged with looking after our health, tried to implement the hydrogenation process today as a new development they would not be able to use it – so why allow it? Simple - Big business needs cosseting or was that the glint of a Mark, Franc or Pound I can see!

Flaxseed oil and flaxseed, which had been part of our staple diet for more than 5000 years, had all but disappeared from our dinner plate. Flax seed's fragile nature of requiring refrigeration, light and heat sensitivity did not suit the mass production techniques and it was much easier for a supermarket to handle packaged products that do not require so much attention - where they only need to pile the shelves high.

The supermarkets need to address some of these issues. They have a duty of care to us as customers and lay-persons who may not fully understand some of the food processes. Making sure products that contain hydrogenated oils or trans fatty acids are clearly marked on the label. Instead of beating down the farmer on price how about ensuring we get excellent nutritious food. My sister recently remarked to me, 'When was the last time you took a bite from an apple and checked to see if there was a maggot inside'. The answer is I do not. Why, because the pesticides used on fruit prevent the maggot forming inside the fruit, yet when I was a child we always checked the apples – especially the ones that had been scrumped!

Modern day stores - large or small and households are now equipped with refrigeration. Transportation and mail order has become efficient one-day deliveries. All of these now allow flaxseed oil and other delicate oils to be stored safely both in the shop and at home. Due to the nitrogen flushing and refrigeration a shelf life of only a couple of days back in the 1950's has now extended to 6 months and with deep freezing that can be increased to 12 months.

A Marriage In Heaven

Dr Johanna Budwig a world-renowned scientist, lecturer and author, originated and developed what is known as the oil-protein diet in Germany and Europe achieving outstanding results with many individuals suffering with chronic debilitating illnesses. Dr Budwig has been nominated for a Nobel Prize for medicine - seven times, having spent more than 50 years describing how unsaturated EFA's (Essential Fatty Acids) when combined with a high quality protein (Cottage Cheese) enables the EFA's to be readily water soluble and metabolised within the body, which will counteract toxic and poisonous accumulations in all tissues of the body.

What Do Our Body's Need!

They need highly unsaturated fats. These fats play a decisive role in almost all body functions and most importantly for respiratory functioning (formation of new cells) of the body which includes generating a field of electrons and recharging of living tissue especially the nerve system and the brain.

What Is Fat?

Fat is known as a lipid and consists of a substance called glycerine. When saturated fats occur naturally in the body these require the presence of Essential Fatty Acid (EFA's) to be turned into energy.

What is an Unsaturated Fat?

Some unsaturated fats and proteins link together and combine in such a way that they have the ability to become water-soluble within the body. Some of the association between highly unsaturated fats and proteins have been research for more than 100 years and have been noted for the unique ability to form these important body functions. Other oils have unsaturated fats such as Olive Oil although not in anyway harmful for us olive oil it is not the most beneficial for people in our temperate climate in Europe (UK, Germany, France and Benelux).

Oil-Protein Combination:
Two Of The Nutrients We Need- *They Also Need Each Other*
Back in the 1800's scientists were on the right track. As early as 1842, many scientists knew there was a definite connection between a healthy body and supplementing the diet daily with an oil and protein combination. One hundred and fifty years ago the reasons for this combination and the benefits were not understood. With technology today and modern scientific developments, the scientists have been able to accurately assess and define the workings of the oil-protein combination on the human system.

Scientists and research workers found results from their experiments, that conclusively proved the combination of oil and protein belong together in nutrition, and work hand in hand in the body. The researchers also found that sensitivity to toxins magnified if oil and protein were not given together, and in the right proportions.

During the early 1900's four Nobel Prize winning scientists took up the challenge to understand the relationship between oil and protein combination and the benefits it had on human health in separate research projects.

Thunberg understood the importance of the sulphur-rich proteins. He also knew that these proteins worked in combination with a functioning partner within the biological system. Meticulously he searched for this partner, but he was unable to discover it due to the apparatus and methodology needed to finish his work had not yet been invented.

Meyerhof found that a two elements within the body, fatty acid linoleic, and sulphur-rich proteins worked well together to assist overstressed and fatigued muscles to recover from exertion and exercise rapidly. unfortunately, it was too early in the world of science to understand that linoleic acid was essential for the human body and thus he did not recognize the far-reaching significance of his work.

Szent-Gyorgyi pushed the science a little further and proved that sulphur-rich proteins, when combined with linoleic acid, take up and transport oxygen throughout the body. As with his predecessors he lacked the biochemical tools to prove the identity of the components

Warburg proved that a fatty substance was required to kick-start the oxidation process when it was low, as is apparent in many chronic illnesses especially cancer and diabetes. He worked on a number of different fatty acids, and was disheartened when the results did not occur as he expected. Warburg was very familiar with linoleic acid, but it had not occurred to him to try it within his experiments.

These four Nobel Prize winners turned their attentions to other scientific work as the technical difficulties in those early days were insurmountable as quantum physics and specialist high-powered microscopes were still some time away. They had nearly solved the problem and the research was put on the scientific back burner for many years.

Picking Up The Pieces

It was not until the 1950's that Dr Budwig with a broad perspective, which included chemistry, quantum physics, biochemistry, pharmacology and medicine picked up the scientific pieces to the jig-saw puzzle and the challenge began.

Dr. Johanna Budwig recognised the obstructions in scientific research that had gone on before, and those that had prevented previous scientists understanding the oil-protein relationship.

Dr. Budwig methodically and meticulously went about the time-consuming work to develop reliable new methods and techniques in biochemistry. Dr Budwig has admitted at her lectures that if it was not for the new science of quantum physics and the evolution and development of new scientific equipment she herself may have never found the answers. Many scientists refer to some of Budwig's ground-breaking techniques; including the development of equipment so sensitive that the fatty constituents from the smallest amount of blood can be accurately separated and the individual substances identified within that droplet.

With these new techniques, Dr. Budwig started to work with the chronically ill and diseased patients. Their daily diet was supplemented with an oil-protein combination. Dr Budwig viewed many natural oil bearing foods that were high in EFA's and eventually settled in using flaxseed oil due to its high concentration of essential fatty acids. Budwig started by combining the flaxseed oil with reduced fat milk because of its sulphurated protein source. Later, substituting the milk with Quark, a low-fat cottage cheese because of the much higher content of sulphur proteins as well as the palatability of this low fat alpine cheese.

Dr. Budwig research findings using the combination of sulphated protein and essential fatty acid is that neither do the job alone, they are needed in combination before the body will assimilate them.

Budwig also found that only in the correct ratio/proportion will the patient gain any benefit. This is due to the fact that the essential fatty acids need to bind to the protein.

Confident in her findings, Dr. Budwig fed seriously ill cancer patients the flaxseed oil and quark combination and monitored the improvements in her patients.

She found a yellowish-green substance in their blood was soon replaced with a healthy red pigment, haemoglobin. The phosphatides began to return and the lipoproteins reappeared. Budwig also found that tumourous lumps receded and disappeared. Anaemia in her patients was alleviated, their vital energy increased and vitality returned - the patients recuperated.

It took about 12 weeks for these changes. During this period, any symptoms of cancer, diabetes, or liver disease also disappeared. Due to her many years of research and important discoveries, Dr. Johanna Budwig has given many thousands of individuals the opportunity to live healthier, longer lives. She is quite rightly revered as the foremost authority on augmenting the daily diet with the essential fatty acids found in flaxseed oil with the companion sulphated proteins.

Taking a trip back to those early days. The populace in Germany were enthusiastic for this almost unbelievable information. Processors of commercial dietary fats (margarine, vegetable oils, and shortening) did not like the findings of Dr Budwig, nor did they sit comfortable with her lectures. These big businessmen went to extreme lengths to try to stop her from publishing her work and its subsequent findings. Initially, Dr Budwig's important dissertations were met with some resistance prompted by those with a fiscal involvement in the commercial fats industry, fortunately her persistence paid off and her work has enlightened other scientists to follow a similar route.

Up until several years ago, Dr Johanna Budwig was lecturing on the adverse reactions in the body of what she refers to as 'pseudo' fats. These lecture are less frequent now due to her age. What she outlined was; the oil manufacturers in order to lengthen the storage or shelf life of their oils and products use chemical processes that render their products harmful to the human body. The products Dr Budwig refers to as 'pseudo' fats are otherwise known as 'hydrogenated oil'. Once fats and oils are subjected to chemical processing the vital electron cloud is destroyed within the fat. By removing the electrons, these fats no longer have the ability to bind with oxygen, becoming a harmful fatty substance that will be deposited within the body. Some vital organs within our body reject or do not identify these fats and as an example the heart will reject these fats and they end as an inorganic fat deposit in the heart muscle.

Those fats that are chemically processed are no longer water-soluble when bound to a protein. These 'pseudo' fats eventually block the circulation, damage cardiovascular action, inhibit (respiration) the renewal of cells and slow the flow of blood and lymph fluids.

To sustain our health, as well as our body's metabolic functions and these functions being bio/chemical/electrical in action need good nutritional oils. If the functions involving cardiovascular, circulation etc are interrupted with excessive pseudo fats they may be slowed down or even entirely completely paralysed.

Nutritional fats such as essential fatty acids (omega-3) are extremely important for man and animal alike. Nutritional and medical science has proved conclusively that the role of fats within our body's are vitally important for the correct metabolism, synthesis or just plain living. Fats (lipids) are used within the metabolic process by our body as well as in all areas of its growth processes. The reserve energy sources in the body are based on the metabolism of fats (lipid). Those growth processes involving fat extend from the renewal of cells (respiration) throughout the body, to brain and nerve function as well as our sensory organs (eyes and ears).

At our body's cellular level, to replace and repair efficiently the cells need pure polyunsaturated, electron-rich oils that can be found in abundance in flaxseed oil High quality, natural polyunsaturated oils absorb oxygen and proteins in huge amounts and then transport their vital cargo throughout the body, visiting each and every organ.

Lipids (fats) in our body can only become water-soluble and mobile when they have been bound to a high quality protein source, therefore the relevance of protein-rich Quark.

If we consumed the combination mentioned earlier, that being an electron-rich fat that is combined with a protein, the electrons within the fat are totally protected until the body needs the energy. The body will then be able to call on this easily accessible energy source immediately on demand, exactly as mother nature intended.

Many scientists from around the world have followed Dr Budwig's lead and some impressive results have begun to flow such as anti-tumour activity, increased metabolic rate, greatly optimised immune system, reduction in blood cholesterol levels, normalisation of blood pressure and inhibition of cancer cell formation.

Research papers and testimonials abound on the health benefits achieved by including unrefined, cold-pressed flaxseed oil combined with quark in a diet. Following almost twenty years of solid therapeutic clinical application, Dr Budwig's original oil-protein diet has proven successful where many conventional remedies have failed. The oil-protein combination has seen use in Europe therapeutically for the prevention and treatment of: arteriosclerosis, arthritis, bronchial spasms and disorders, cancer, cardiac infarction, eczema (aids all skin diseases), fatty degeneration of the liver, hypertrophic prostate, irregular heartbeat, irregular intestinal activity, stomach ulcers, strokes, afflictions of old age, reduced brain activity, immune system deficiency syndromes such as multiple sclerosis and autoimmune illnesses.

The Omega-3 Protein Diet that follows later has been updated since Dr Budwig's original masterful combination. Research has moved forward, new components in flaxseed have been found that reinforce Dr Budwig's original theories.

One of today's the leading research scientists, Professor Lillian Thompson of University of Toronto has spent 15 years researching the nutritional and cancer related benefits of flaxseed. Professor Thompson's along with Dr Johanna Budwig's work gave me the confidence to proceed along the 'flax road' to improved health.

What The Doctor's, Experts & Media Say!

16th International Congress of Nutrition Montreal - July 1997.

Dr Stephen Cunnane, Professor, Dept of Nutritional Sciences, University of Toronto. Chairperson said: "Flax seed has beneficial effects in the prevention of cancer, coronary heart disease (CHD) and sudden death from heart arrhythmias".

Dr Alexander Leaf MD, Professor Emeritus, Dept of Medicine, Harvard University. Says. "There are annually 500,000 CHD related deaths in the USA" – Dr Leaf's findings suggested: "Half of those cases die within one hour from fatal arrhythmias and this may be prevented with Omega-3 – alpha linolenic acid - as found in flax seed oil, is effective in preventing arrhythmias caused when an artery is clogged and the heart muscle cannot be fed with blood".

Dr Walter Willet, Harvard University: reiterated Dr Leaf's findings by saying: "Studies have consistently found almost 50% lower risk of fatal CHD, with only a slight increase in an intake of alpha-linolenic acid (ALA)".

Dr Lillian U. Thompson, Professor, Dept of Nutritional Sciences, Faculty of Medicine, University of Toronto said: "flaxseed has tremendous potential to positively affect our health".

Phipps W, et al, Journal Clinical Endocrinol Metab, 77(5), 1993. "Our data suggest a significant specific role for lignans (as in flax seed) in relationship between diet and sex steroid action, and possibly between diet and the risk of breast and other hormonally dependent cancers".

Obermeyer W, et al. U.S. Food and Drug Admin, Center for Food Safety and Applied Nutrition. Fed Am Soc Exp Biol, A863, 1993.

"Flaxseed lignans have antitumour, antimototic, antioxidant and weak estrogenic activities, are potentially the richest source of phytoestrogens in the human diet and may be linked to a low incidence of breast and colon cancer".

Professor Lillian U. Thompson, et al, Carcinogenesis, 17:1373, 1996. "Flaxseed, a rich source of mammalian lignan precursors secoisolariciresinol-diglycoside (SD [SDG]) and alpha-linolenic acid (ALA), has been shown to be protective at the early promotion stage of carcinogenesis. In conclusion, the SD lignans in flaxseed appears to be beneficial throughout the promotional phase of carcinogenesis whereas the oil (high lignan only) component is more effective at the stage when tumours have already been established".

Prasad K, Atherosclerosis, 132(1): 69, 1997. "Modest dietary flax seed supplementation is effective in reducing hyper-cholesterolemic atherosclerosis markedly without lowering serum cholesterol. Dietary flax seed supplementation could, therefore, prevent hypercholesterolemia-related heart attack and strokes".

Li D, et al, Cancer Lett, 142(1): 91, 1999. "Dietary supplementation with SDG, a lignan precursor isolated from flax seed, significantly reduced pulmonary metastasis of melanoma cells and inhibited the growth of metastatic tumours that formed in the lungs".

Euro. Urology, 35(5-6): 377, 1999. "Plant lignans give rise to the mammalian lignans, enterodiol and enterolactone; the richest source is flax seed. In addition to their estrogenic activity, these plant compounds can interfere with the steroid metabolism and bio-availability, and also inhibit enzymes, such as kinase and topoisomerase, which are crucial to cellular proliferation and hence may contribute to lower incidences of prostate cancer".

Weight Watchers® the International Diet Organisation has recently elevated flaxseed to number 1 in it's chart of most nutritional food.

The Food Programme on BBC 4 Radio: On the 14th October 2001 the BBC broadcast a 30 minute programme highlighting the benefits of essential fatty acids and omega-3 and the undesirable excessive amounts of omega-6 in our bodies.

Getting To Know Flax Seed

Wherever flax seed becomes a regular food item among the people, there will be better health. Mahatma Gandhi

Flaxseed also known as Linseed has been grown for more than 5000 years for human nutrition and food source. The finest of this highly nutritious seed are grown on the open prairies of Canada. There are two types of nutritional food flax seeds. The brown (red/brown) is grown on the Western Prairies of Canada and there is also the golden flax seed that is generally grown further south on the plains of South and North Dakota. Brown flax seed from Canada is slightly higher both in oil content and a better nutritional value. There are several reasons for the difference in these seeds but mainly the growing conditions of the Western Plains of Canada particularly suit the flax plant, thereby producing very high quality seed.

The whole flax seed is almost half made up of nutritionally rich oils, the remainder consisting of fibre, complete amino acid proteins and mucilage and a wealth of nutrients. Flax oil, when extracted with care is Mother Nature's greatest source of essential fatty acids and cancer fighting lignans known to man. The proteins in flax seeds are easily digested and contain the full array of complete amino acids needed for repairing and building a strong body and an optimised immune system. The fibre in flax is of tremendous benefit to a toxic colon acting as a broom it sweeps away any toxic material, metabolic waste material and dried mucus. Flax seed fibre is a perfect food for friendly bacteria in the intestines helping to eliminate disease-causing organisms at bay.

A little over 12% of flax seed consists of mucilage a gum like substance that makes it a non-irritating, gentle, natural laxative. The mucilage of flax seed acts as a buffer for excess stomach acids, it is perfect for those who have a sensitive stomach, where it can sooth ulcers an irritable bowel. Flax seed expands up to 20 times in volume and absorbs 8 times its own weight in fluid when in the body. Flaxseed should be taken with a generous amount of water (150ml to 1 tablespoon of milled or whole seed).

The whole flax seed slowly releases its mucilage through the seed case or fibre wall. If you intend soaking the whole seeds within 30 minutes the small red-brown seeds will form a slippery mucilage. They will act as tiny mucilage release capsules. This release continues, changing the water to a consistency similar to a light oil.

Flax seed contain lignans that have anti-viral, anti-bacterial, anti-fungal and anti-cancer properties. Flax seeds have the richest source of lignans, 100 times more than the next best source, wheat bran. The majority of lignans are found in the whole seed, giving it an advantage over flax oil, although the oil is essential for two very important essential fatty acids (EFA's). Flax seed also contains lecithin, which emulsifies fat and cholesterol and is important in maintaining a healthy nervous system and preventing stress in the body. Taking flaxseed daily enables lecithin to work slowly on fat deposits in the body and remove unnecessary fats. These little red-brown seeds improve digestion, help stabilize blood glucose levels, aid in fighting tumour formation and enhance cardiovascular health.

Flax Oil

Flax oil is worth getting very excited about. It is considered the most nutritious of all the oils in the world, containing generous amounts of the two essential fatty acids our body needs to function properly.

Flax seeds are equipped with a hard, tough outer case. This casing protects the fragile and delicate oils within. Eating flax seeds whole, it would be impossible for your body to draw on any of the vital nutrients within the seed. In fact, even after the seeds pass through the digestive track, they can still sprout and grow. It is only by preparing, grinding and milling the seed fresh or pressing in a cold-expeller press can we receive the wealth of nutrients hidden inside. Flaxseed oil is Mother Nature's highest source of unsaturated alpha linolenic acid (Omega 3). Many people's diets are lacking in this essential oil. Flax oil also contains Carotene and vitamin E, which are valuable antioxidants.

Inside Flaxseed – What You Will Find

Flaxseed is being re-discovered all over again and is now being described by leading research scientists as the wonder grain of the new millennium, although it has been around for thousands of years.

The nutritional benefits of flaxseed are probably the most impressive of any natural food.

Inside Each Flaxseed You Will Find:
- Flax contains natural anti-oxidants that will keep the oil fresh until they are used up.
- Flax seed is rich in Lecithin, Vitamins B1, B2, C, E, Phospholipids and Carotene.
- Flaxseed contains 12% mucilage a polysaccharide, and is regarded as one of the finest natural laxative you could take without the discomfort of diarrhoea.
- Flaxseed also has beneficial effects on an acidic stomach and lowers cholesterol level by preventing the re-absorption of bile.
- The ratio of soluble to insoluble fibre is an impressive 40-60%. NCI (National Cancer Institute) recommends 25-35g per day of fibre.
- Flaxseed contains up to 9.2mg of potassium per gram, around 5 to 10 fold than that of raw bananas, without the sugar level of banana.
- Flaxseed contains 100 fold more Lignans than the next nearest natural source, wheat bran.
- A tablespoon (15ml) of milled or ground flaxseed contains up to 3800mg of ALNA, the primary, elemental Omega-3. This is 10 fold higher than of most fish oil capsules without the risks such as rancid taste, chemical residues, high cholesterol and saturated fat level.
- Flaxseed is a prominent disease fighter with such illnesses as arthritis, atherosclerosis, cancer, lupus nephritis and diabetes. Professor Lillian Thompson of University of Toronto and researchers at the Saskatoon Research Centre in Canada have identified and developed the technology to

extract a valuable lignan compound from flaxseed called SDG, this is the little beauty that fights many of the unwanted degenerative diseases mentioned earlier. SDG has been identified as a phytochemical and is tongue twistingly entitled Secoisolariciresinol Diglucoside. It is found in the whole seed or defatted flax meal.
- Flaxseed has nature's highest source of Omega 3 an EFA (essential fatty acid). Omega 3 is traditionally associated with supplements of Cod Liver Oil, but flaxseed has twice the amount of this valuable component, without possible contaminates.

The Fats That Heal Us

Prior to my illness I was among many other individuals who did not understand why 'fats' have such an important if not vital association with our body's metabolism. Most, if not all of the important metabolic processes essential for healthy living require fat. Neither do many individuals understand that these should be the correct fats and in the correct ratio. Most people have heard of Omega-3, which in the UK is normally associated with Cod Liver Oil. Omega-3 is a fat – all but an extremely vital and essential fat for our body.

EFAs (essential fatty acids) are vital nutrients that our body's and we need in much larger quantities than we are currently ingesting, not in tiny milligram amounts but in several spoonful servings every day.

For our body to function normally we need 50 or so vital nutrients and two of these are **essential fatty acids (EFA's)**. These two EFA's are from a family of fats and oils that are sometimes referred to as super-polyunsaturated oils. One of these EFA's is alpha-linolenic acid abbreviated to (ALA) and more commonly referred to as Omega-3; the other is linoleic acid (LA) and is referred to as Omega-6. Both are very delicate, fragile oils and require a great deal of care during the cold expeller pressing, packaging and delivery. They are easily destroyed by UV light, oxygen and high temperature, which would make them toxic to the body. *The sources section gives the best supply source.*

Digestive System
The seat of our digestion and most important organ in our body is the liver. The liver thrives on Omega-3. Other vital inner organs, the kidneys, pancreas and adrenal glands, all need EFAs to function effectively, as do our cells, tissue and other glands in the body.
Flaxseed has the benefit of cleansing and aiding the intestinal and digestive track. With an efficient working digestive system you will be receiving all the goodness from your food.

Immune
Our immune system, metabolism and the cells that make up our immune response require EFA's to produce hydrogen peroxide (oxygen) which our body's use so that we can defeat infectious bacteria, toxins, foreign invaders and illness. EFAs protect our DNA and our genetic material from damage. EFA's are the lorries that transport oxygen around our body's pathways via the roadways, our blood. EFA's dominate in the metabolising of proteins and minerals. EFA's are our lifeline to survival, both health and well being.

Fighting the Invaders
The poor old overworked EFAs assist the body in fighting fungi, mutagens, carcinogens, bacteria, toxin removal and infections such as candida. No wonder we need spoonfuls of EFA's they have not finished there job yet - with their side kicks the lignans, they get to work by inhibiting tumour growth *(National Cancer Institute: Research, USA).*

Cardiovascular Aid - And A Lot More
A fat that reduces blood fats! Is that not remarkable?
You bet it is – But then that is exactly what Mother Nature intended! This is only one of the remarkable attributes of the

humble flaxseed. With EFAs properly balanced in our diet they produce prostaglandin hormones, absolutely vital for good health. As well as many other functions prostaglandins make blood platelets less sticky by making them more slippery, which in turn reduces the likelihood of a clot forming in an artery to a vital organ, such as your brain or heart, thus protecting you from strokes, angina and heart attacks. By making the blood more viscous the heart is not overloaded this in turn aids in lowering high blood pressure. Then the regal EFAs help your kidneys remove excess water and reduce inflammation throughout the body. Now do you believe why they're so over worked and why we need much more of them than we are currently ingesting.

Energy production
Anyone regularly using fresh flaxseed oil and flaxseed flake will notice his or her energy levels pick up. Their physical activity increases, they have more stamina available, get tired less quickly, recover faster from exertion or physical training. This energy transformation is not a quick fix like you get from a cup of tea, coffee or caffeine supplement, but a sustained, stable and extended energy.
EFAs increase oxidation in the body. EFA's stoke and stroke the metabolic processes. EFAs transport oxygen to the vital cells and tissue, which in turn increases energy levels and stamina for active sports persons, athletes, the aged and the obese. Athletic prowess and performance is enhanced both in endurance and strength critical sports. EFAs speed recovery from fatigue and muscle injury.

Skin, Hair And Nails
With such a humble little seed how is it able to do all of this?
The Omega-3 works away by visiting every cell, tissue and organ within the body. So when the EFA find something wrong in the body they try to put it right. In turn it will be responsible for improving and producing pliable, smooth and velvety skin. Hair will develop sheen, become silky and smooth. Nails will be less

prone to splitting grow faster and stronger. The regal EFAs identify those parts of our body that are not as they would want them to be, so they try and put them right, not once but over and over again. This all happens from within, there is no need to oil your skin from the outside.

Using the right amounts of properly balanced, properly processed EFA rich oils you'll be the envy of your friends. Healthy adults usually require 2 tablespoons of flaxseed oil and 2 tablespoons of fresh ground seed per day.

What To Look Out For
- Dry or flaky skin indicates a need for EFAs.
- Individuals also tan better and burn less.
- You body uses more EFA in the colder months than in summer - supplement more in the winter.
- Dry skin is inconvenient. A dry liver or brain is deadly.
- Our vital organs get priority on the EFAs ingested.
- EFAs enter the tissue and aid in forming a protective barrier in our skin. In doing so we get relief from eczema, acne, psoriasis and other skin disorders.

Weight loss, loss, loss, loss, loss
- EFAs increase the metabolic rate in our body; allowing us to burn off more calories.
- EFAs aid in the kidneys function in removing excess water from our tissues, which accounts for additional weight in some individuals.
- EFAs aid in decreasing cravings for certain fats (chocolate) that are as a result from not receiving the nutrients we need.
- EFAs induce calmness, elevate mood and lift depressions, another reason why some individual over eat.

Brain Development And Brain Function

As I mentioned earlier our vital organs require EFAs to work efficiently, none more so than our brain and our little 'grey cells'. The organ richest in EFAs is our brain with more than half of its weight consisting of electron rich fat. A properly balanced diet containing EFA rich oils and freshly prepared flax seed, will benefit children with learning difficulties or bad adolescent behaviour by aiding the transmission of the electrical signals in the brain. Electric signals through and from the brain are more precise, we become more alert, and less stressed which allows us to cope with the fast society we live in. By balancing the Omega-3 in expectant mothers it aids in developing visual and neurological parts of the foetus.

Mental Illness
Many depressed people would benefit from improved intake and balance of EFAs. EFAs are key nutrients for treating mental conditions and a properly balanced intake of EFAs for schizophrenics will result in less hallucination. EFAs are a positive benefit in lifting depression and elevating mood. EFAs induce calmness.

Reproductive
Omega 3 is a precursor in the production process of hormone within our body's. Sperm formation requires EFAs to complete this important process. EFAs also aid in preventing pre-menstrual syndrome.

It is estimated that in Britain most of the population may be up to 90% deficient in Omega-3.

Not Just A Number - Uniquely Omega-3,

Flax seed oil is approximately twice as concentrated in Omega-3 essential fatty acids over the next richest source, the fish oils (Cod Liver Oil). Flaxseed, particularly the brown seed from Canada has a content of 43% to 45% of nutritious oil in the seed. Over half of that oil is Omega-3, having an average of 55-60%.

When we are healthy and well and with optimum conditions within the tissues and cells of our body, alpha-linolenic acid (ALA), which is the parent Omega-3 in flax seed oil is changed by our body's enzymes via a catalytic conversion to special longer-chain, Omega-3 Fatty Acids. These new acids are primarily EPA (eicosapentaenoic acid) as found in Cod Liver Oil and DHA (docosahexaenoic acid).

Therefore, **ALA, EPA, and DHA** - make up the Omega-3 fatty acid family in humans.

DHA is by far the most complex fatty acid of the Omega-3 family and is perhaps the most important of this EFA family for human health. For our brain to function correctly we need DHA to be fed regularly to which enables visual sharpness, learning processes, memory, cognition, behaviour responses, decision making and almost all mental activity and it also plays a vital role for cell membrane function and our homeostatis overall.

DHA, when synthesised in the body is an extremely long-chain molecule, however, several enzymatic reactions are required to metabolise it from ALA (Omega 3). The enzymes involved are the same as those necessary for the Omega-6 EFA conversion - we'll deal with Omega 6 (LA) later.

There are more than 100,000 metabolic processes and reactions within our body that determine the function and structure of our cell membranes and almost all of them depend on EFAs for these vitally important processes. EFAs are in the starting blocks for the essential metabolic reaction for the production of prostaglandins (PGs) – hormone like substances that acts as messengers balancing the entire organ system and balancing the homeostatic status of our body. Research findings have found that optimum health and well being is directly related to optimum prostaglandin balance, which in turn is controlled by the types, ratio and amounts of fatty acids that are acquired as part of our diet. The Omega-3 hierarchy of EFAs is required by our body in relatively large amounts, if not, deficiency is characterised initially by irritability, impatience, a pale/light and dry or flaking of the skin, and certain systemic nervous and visual problems.

Indications For Supplementation
With the modern domination of refined and processed foods in our diet, coupled with the widespread use of hydrogenated oils and margarines, it is likely that the average diet, is barely borderline in respect to the sufficiency of EFAs in our body.
Deficiency can manifest itself in many ways when you consider how important EFAs are within our body. If the vital organs require EFAs before anything else then certain functions of the body may begin to show signs of stress or dysfunction before chronic illness sets in. If there is a continual deficiency of EFAs then eventually the vital organs will be waving the old white flag in surrender, by that time chronic illness has already started.
Some of the problem is the balance of EFA's. Research findings in the USA has indicated that some areas of the population can be up to 80% deficient in (ALA) Omega-3 and over burdened with (LA) Omega 6 by ingesting too much of the wrong fats or oils. A recent study revealed that a typical 'fast food' diet showed a ratio of 13:1 with regards to the relationship in our body of Omega-6 to Omega-3 – The correct ratio should be about 5:1, so we do need more Omega-3 to compensate. Also with the ingestion of hydrogenated oils and trans fatty acids, these horrid fats compete with the EFAs (Omega-3), which further undermines nutrition and health.
With any imbalance or deficiency adverse reactions can occur to the bio-chemical change of Omega-3 to DHA due to the desaturase enzymes that help produce the DHA from ALA (Omega 3) – these can become damaged by:
- Diets high in saturated fats
- Aging
- Alcohol intake

- Tobacco
- Stress
- Some processed foods containing hydrogenated oils and trans fatty acids
- Refined Sugars
- Cholesterol.

Stress may also be a serious culprit and a factor contributing to functional EFA deficiency. These enzymes also become clogged up by (TFA) trans-isomer fatty acids that are abundant in heat processed (hydrogenated) cooking oils, margarines and spreads. As a result of this dysfunctional activity in some of our tissues, including the skin, the circulating army of white cells and platelets, lack the activity necessary to make longer chain fatty acids, they must then rely on the circulation to obtain them.

As we are already ingesting far too much Omega-6 from vegetable oils such as sunflower seed oils, we need to increase our intake of Omega-3.

What Is Flax Seed
Modern Nutrition - Ancient Grain

Flax seed has been consumed since ancient times, and evidence of its health and nutritional benefits are plentiful. Flax seed spread across Europe, Africa and Asia almost 1000 years ago. Charlemagne, King of the Franks and Holy Roman Emperor introduced laws to ensure every one within his Empire grew and ate flax to maintain health. If food were available then it was not difficult to eat healthily in those ancient times. Pesticides, herbicides and preservatives were many hundreds of years away. Food was natural, fresh and wholesome, they understood in those days when food was rancid or stale. Those animals that were domesticated were reared on grasses that filled their flesh with nourishing vitamins and minerals. Wild game as today had a natural diet scavenging for their food.

Grains and crops were grown on soils that were abundant with nutrients. Now, it's a little more difficult. Our modern industrialised society has much to answer for in the 21st Century, we have to encounter heavy refinement of foods and what we are asked to eat is calorie rich but nutritionally devoid of important vital vitamins, minerals, oils and enzymes so necessary for a healthy functioning body. Our soils have been eroded of the important organic nutrients and minerals due to excessive crop growing. On the face of it everything looks rather bleak. The results are diseases that are not genetic in origin, but the direct result of poor dietary and lifestyle choices. A recent European study involving 500,000 individuals from 9 countries, directly linked nutritional deficiency to a third of all cancer related illnesses. However, all is not lost as we still have the abundantly nutrient rich flax seed. Many of the essential nutrients that our bodies have been deficient in are now being liberated from this humble seed.

Nutritional Super Heavyweight
Whole fresh ground flax seed and defatted flax flake; consist of a vast storehouse of nutrients. Locked within the cell matrix of the

flaxseed exists a wealth of nutritional superstars. Leading organic oil processors such as Stone Mills Organic Oils use specialist-milling process to delicately liberate the naturally occurring amino acids, lignans, vitamins, phytonutrients and minerals, without damaging the delicate Omega-3 oils.
The National Cancer Institute (NCI) has evaluated and described flax seed as a component food. 'Foods may be defined as those that composed of one of more ingredients that contribute essential nutrients for health and protect against specific diseases such as cancer and coronary heart disease'.

The finding of their research was no less than remarkable.
NCI Evaluation of Flaxseed As Functional Food
In 1989 the National Cancer Institute of America released millions of dollars in research grants including the Clinical Research Branch of Federal Drug Administration, University of Toronto, South Dakota State University, Midwest Research Institute and others.

Four years later the researchers revealed their findings:
- Levels of 1.25 to 2.5% flax in the diet stimulated the immune system.
- Flax increased vitamin D levels and increased the retention of calcium, magnesium, and phosphate.
- Ground Flaxseed had no negative effects on the liver or intestinal tract and did not lower blood vitamin E levels.
- Flax is high in phytonutrients (lignans) that have anti tumour properties and may be linked to a low incidence of breast and colon cancer.
- Flax contains a high level of Vitamin E an antioxidant at about 800 to 900ppm (parts per million).
- Adding 8% flax to the diet could help diabetic conditions caused by a high fat diet.
- Moderately high levels of flax compared to the same level of oat bran, was better at lowering triglycerides, total

cholesterol and LDL and had favourable effects on insulin activity.

Natural Nutrition Source

We are beginning to live more non-organic lives; everything around us is becoming increasingly more synthetic. A world of man-made vitamins and related supplements predominate. The advantage of flax seed and flake is that firstly it is natural. Second it is wholesome and free of pesticides and herbicides and lastly flax seed and flake provides a comprehensive profile of natural, organically sourced vitamins, major and trace minerals with a full compliment of amino acids.

Nutrients that are derived from natural sources and in appropriate proportion are more readily absorbed metabolised and utilised by the body. Many of these nutrients are found in small quantities in the flax flake and flax seed oil, but scientists have proved that in respect to some of these nutrients taken in the correct proportions we do not need heaps of them, more like micrograms.

As well as a wealth of important nutrients, flax flake and flax seed oil boast the highest natural source of Omega-3 along with dietary fibre, protein, lignans, mucilage, and phenolic compounds.

These are possible factors in reducing risk of arthritis, allergies, cardiovascular disease, hypercholesterolemia, stroke, diabetes, cancer, and at least 40 or more other diseases and illness.

Phytochemicals such as SDG have been identified as lignans in whole flax seed and flax flake with research findings indicating that these may interfere with the development of breast, prostate, colon and other cancerous tumours in humans.

The viscous nature of soluble fibres such as flax seed mucilage is believed to slow down digestion and the absorption of starch from our diet. This slowing down process enables a gradual and sustained release with lower levels of blood glucose, insulin and other endocrine responses. In one study, blood glucose response was almost 30% less for breakfast meals that included flax seed bread. Flax seed consumption (50g/day for 4 wk) by young healthy adults and by the elderly has been shown to increase the number of bowel movements per week by up to a third.

Unique Nutritional Attributes of Whole and Milled Flaxseed

Fibre - Contains both soluble and insoluble dietary fibre
Fatty Acids - Contains essential Omega-3 and 6 as well as non-essential Omega-9 in an excellent balance to support health
Vitamins - Contains 8 essential vitamins
Minerals - Contains 4 major minerals and 4 trace minerals
Tocopherols - Contains alpha, delta, gamma tocopherols
Amino Acids - Contains all 10 essential amino acids (complete protein) as well as 8 non-essential amino acids
Phytochemicals - Contains: Lignans, Phenolic Acids, Flavonoids and Phytic Acid.

Whole Seed – What's It Got?

The contents of the table following indicates the typically the level of EFA's, nutrients, minerals, amino acids, vitamins and trace elements naturally present in whole flax seed.

unsaturates EFA	Vitamins	Major Minerals	Phyto-Nutrients	Amino Acids (Protein)	
Super Poly-	C	Calcium	Lignans	Alanine	Lysine
Omega-3	B-1	Magnesium	Phenolic Acid	Arginine	Methionine
Omega-6	B-2	Phosporus	Flavonoid	Aspartic Acid	Phenyl Alanine
	B-6	Potassium	Phytic Acid	Cystine	Proline
Mono-	Pantothenic Acid	Trace Minerals	Secoisolariciresinol Diglucoside-SDG	Glutamic Acid Glycine	Serine Threonine
Omega-9	Folic Acid	Copper		Histidine	Tryprophan
	Niacin	Iron & Zinc		Isoleucine	Tyrosine
		Manganese		Leucine	Valine

REFERENCES

Serraino M and Thompson LU: The effect of flaxseed on early risk markers for mammary carcinogenesis. Cancer Letters 60:135-42, 1991.

Serraino M and Thompson LU: Flaxseed supplementation and early markers of colon carcinogenesis. Cancer Letters 63:159-65, 1992.

Dieken H: Use of Flaxseed as a Source of Omega 3 Fatty Acids in Humans: Proceedings of the 54th Annual Flax Proceedings, 1-5, Jan 1992

Cunane SC (ed.): Symposium Proceedings: Third Toronto Essential Fatty Acid Workshop on alpha-Linolenic Acid in Human Nutrition and Disease. May 17-18, 1991, Simopoulos AP: Omega-3 fatty acids in health and disease and in growth and development. Am J Clin Nutr 54:438-63, 1991.

Chan JK, Bruce VM and McDonald BE: Dietary-alpha-linolenic acid is as effective as oleic acid and linoleic acid in lowering blood cholesterol in normal lipidemic men. Am J Clin Nutr 53:1230-4, 1991.

Belch JF, et al.: Effects of altering dietary essential fatty acids on requirements for non-steroidal anti-inflammatory drugs in patients with rheumatoid arthritis: a double blind placebo controlled study. Ann Rheum Dis 47:96-104, 1988.

University of Toronto, Toronto, Ontario, Canada. Nutrition 7:435-46, 1991.

Sourcing, Preparing and Storing Flax Seed

It is very important that flaxseed is purchased and stored correctly which will ensure a nutritious healthy product.

Flax seed: Whole flax seed has a shelf life of 1 to 2 years at normal room temperature.

Ground or Cracked Flax Seed: When storing flaxseed that has been cracked, milled or ground, it should be stored in a cool dark place and then once opened it MUST be refrigerated to prevent the oils contained in the seed becoming rancid and consumed within 4 weeks.

Flax seed oil: When purchasing flax seed oil it is best to buy oils that are displayed on a refrigerated shelf or in a very cool ambient temperature. Once opened flaxseed oil MUST be refrigerated and consumed within 4 weeks. If the flax oil bottle has been nitrogen flushed and is unopened and stored in a refrigerated environment, flaxseed oil has a shelf life of 6 months.

How Do I Know The Oil I Bought Is Safe: A good indication of the freshness of flax seed oil is by taste. Flax seed oil should have a nutty flavour. If the oil has a slight bitter or fishy taste then you can assume the oil has become rancid.

What To Buy: Flax seed oil should be cold pressed, pesticide free and in an opaque or a UV inhibitor container. It also benefits the consumer if the bottle states that it has been nitrogen flushed. The sooner the oil is consumed from pressing the higher the nutritional benefits. Flax seed oil that is lignan rich has a mid to dark brown colour when shaken. The best whole seed to purchase is the Canadian selected grade 1 seed. These are a chocolate brown colour and I use them in preference to the yellow/golden seed. This type of seed and oil is available from Stone Mills Organic Oils and can be bought direct from the factory and delivered to your door within 24 hours of coming off the press.

What Do I Need To Take?

Table 1 shown on page 49 indicates the approximate daily amounts of flaxseed oil, seed and sulphated protein. It is recommended to ingest flaxseed oil combined with a sulphated protein such as Yoghurt, Cottage Cheese or Quark. This has many additional benefits over taking the oil alone. Also if you wish to receive the full benefits from SDG (a special phytochemical) you must include in your diet no less than two tablespoons of fresh ground flaxseed every day.

If you are involved daily at a level of professional sports, heavy continual manual work or suffering with a chronic ailment or illness you should consider looking at your entire diet, especially for the unwell, this should be assessed by a health care professional or nutritionist who understands the healing benefits of flaxseed.

Summary:
Flaxseed Oil, Ground Whole Flaxseed or Flake – should be part of your regular daily diet.
Flaxseed Oil: To receive the full 'firecracker' benefits from flaxseed oil it should be taken with a good quality sulphur bearing protein as mentioned. *Refer to _-Protein Diet.*

It is important to take at least one glass of water (150ml to 1 tablespoon of flake) following the ingestion of Flax Flake. Flax Flake absorbs its own weight in water to a ratio of 8:1.

Table 1 below represents an INDICATION only of the amount of High Lignan Flax Seed Oil, Ground Whole Flax Seed or Flake that should be consumed daily. If you are suffering with an underlying illness or medical condition it is important that you inform your professional medical carer or doctor of any major changes in your diet.

High Lignan Flaxseed Oil and Flaxseed Flake are natural foods and there are no known adverse reactions when taken alongside prescription medications.

It is recommended that where any ailment or illness is involved a full dietary and nutritional plan be put in place. Additional information can be obtained from Lignan Nutritional, details you will find in the sources section.

Table 1

	Servings per day	Flaxseed Oil Serving	Quark Serving	Or, Yoghurt Serving	Flax Flake/ Seed
Child under 12 yr	1	1 Tsp		40g	1 tsp
Adults-Preventative	1	2 Tbsp	60g	80g	2 Tbsp
Pregnancy & Lactation	1	1-2 Tbsp	30g-60g	40g-80g	2 Tbsp
Athletes & Sports	2	2 Tbsp	60g	80g	2 Tbsp
Ailments	2	2 Tbsp	60g	80g	2 Tbsp
Chronic Illness	3	2 Tbsp	60g	80g	3 Tbsp
Cancer	3	2 Tbsp	60g	80g	3 Tbsp
Diabetes I	3	2 Tbsp	60g	80g	3 Tbsp
Diabetes II	2	2 Tbsp	60g	80g-125g	3 Tbsp
Heart Infarction,	2	2 Tbsp	60g	80g-125g	3 Tbsp
Notes:					
My Supplements					

How To Take Flaxseed Oil

Flaxseed oil has a pleasant nutty flavour. The only objection some individuals have with taking the oil is that it an oil. Flaxseed oil is beneficial to anybody young or old and even the couch potato may benefit, the active sports person definitely will.

Flaxseed Oil may be added to your favourite fruit juice. Put two tablespoons of oil into a glass top up with juice and drink straight down. The oil is so pure it leaves no after taste. For those individuals who want to improve upon their existing good health it is recommended that you take two tablespoons per day of oil and two tablespoons of ground whole flaxseed.

For those who are unwell it is recommended in following one of the diet plans suggested in later chapters. What must be considered is the level of omega-3 required to assist with your particular ailment. There is a plateau where upon until you reach that amount of oil each day, little or no benefit will be received from the flaxseed oil… why…there are so many

Ground Whole Flaxseed

Ground flaxseed has some extra special nutrients not found in the pressed oil. The oil is needed to reverse the omega-3 deficiency we find in our diet. The seed has many other benefits as you will read later.

With a coffee mill grind the seed to a course powder. You can now add the seed to your favourite, cereal, porridge, soup or beverage. Only used fresh ground seed.

Allow to stand for a minute or two.

Always drink a glass of water following the seed.

The seed is a natural mild laxative and is of particular benefit to any individual suffering with an ailment to the intestines, colon or bowel.

Rules For A Healthy Body

Maintaining a healthy body involves some simple health enhancing rules. By adhering to the following recommendations there is a greater chance of you winning your next marathon race or fighting off chronic illness.

Your Food – Many processed foods contain unnatural substances including additives, preservatives and modified or altered oils that are detrimental to the body. Most of the additives in processed foods inhibit the immune system and by continuing to consume a large proportion of your diet with processed foods it will delay or even prevent recovery from illness. For a sports person processed food degrades the metabolism, reduces oxygen intake, respiration and recovery from strenuous exercise.

Fresh fruit and vegetables should be cleaned and washed thoroughly before preparation and ingestion and in preference should be organic wherever possible.

For continual health and fitness, proteins, fats and carbohydrates must be in balance. Nutritional recommendations vary greatly from individual to individual, but about 20% to 25% of your calories should be made up from fats, but the correct fats.

The Biochemists first rule:

'Fats Burn In The Flame Of Carbohydrates'

So make sure you have adequate carbohydrates to burn off any excess fats.

How Much Protein Is Enough?

In the tables that follow you will see protein intake levels ranging from one gram of protein to two grams of protein per kilogram of body weight - that's a 100% difference - it is important to remember the level of protein is determined by the level of exercise and physical work you inflict on your body.

Discovering Your Daily Protein Intake

From *Table 1,* find the number that closely matches your activity level. Then with either *chart 2* or *chart 3* find your ideal body weight - follow this row across until you find the column figure that you established in *Table1* (Your activity level value). You will now have a total figure of the amount of protein you should consume in a day.

That's how easy it is to determine the protein you need each day.

Activity Level Table
Table 1: Grams of Protein per day to kgs of body weight.

Value gm/kg	Activity Level
1.0	Sedentary, no sport or fitness exercise
1.2	Jogging or light fitness training
1.4	Activity sports or training 3 times a week
1.6	Moderate training every day, aerobic or weights
1.8	Heavy weight training daily - one session a day
2.0	Heavy weight training daily plus sports training, or two-sessions a day weight training

Example: If you are a regular jogger or train three times a week and had to lay off for several days with an injury it is advisable to reduce the protein intake to the level below your normal daily intake. If you work in an occupation where your workload is physical throughout the working day, then your protein intake should be towards the higher level.

Ideal Body Weight Charts:

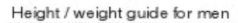

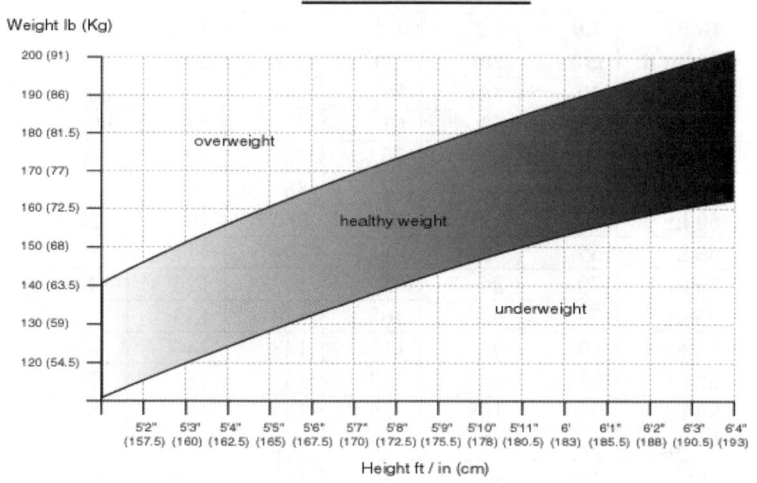

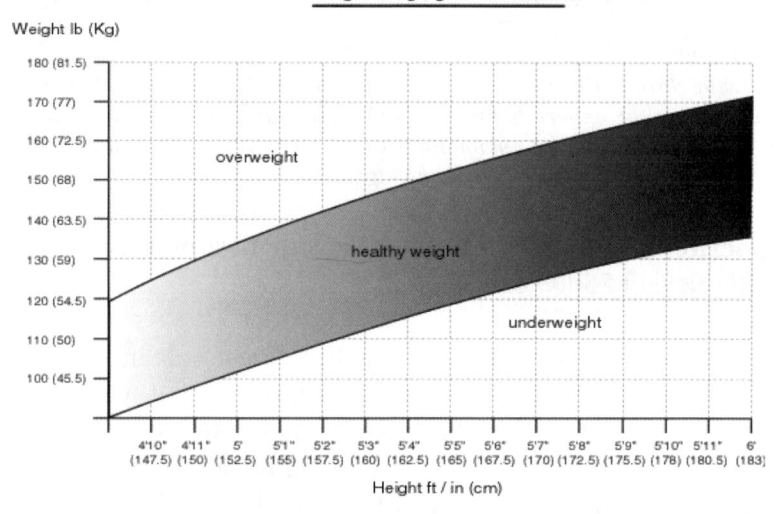

Daily Protein Intake Table
Table 4:

Body Weight fl	1.0 gm	1.2 gm	1.4 gm	1.6 gm	1.8 gm	2.0 gm
40 kg	40	48	56	64	72	80
45 kg	45	54	63	72	81	90
50 kg	50	60	70	80	90	100
55 kg	55	66	77	88	99	110
60 kg	60	72	84	96	108	120
65 kg	65	78	91	104	117	130
70 kg	70	84	98	112	126	140
75 kg	75	90	105	120	135	150
80 kg	80	96	112	128	144	160
85 kg	85	102	119	136	153	170
90 kg	90	108	126	144	162	180
95 kg	95	114	133	152	171	190
100 kg	100	120	140	160	180	200
105 kg	105	126	147	168	189	210
110 kg	110	132	154	176	198	220

Important note:
For those with chronic illnesses and especially cancer it is important that you consult a nutritional expert before embarking on any significant dietary changes. It is very important to maintain a stable body weight. Your diet must be balanced. For further advice contact the Lignan Centre Ltd

As Hypocrites remarked: "Let food be your first medicine"
- It is still relevant 2500 years later.

Digestion – Even if you consume the finest, cleanest and healthiest food available, if your digestion is not working properly, then you are either throwing money down the toilet or you are not converting your food into the enzymes and minerals your body needs. Poor digestion is often signalled by flatulence or wind. As we pass 30 or so years of age our acidic digestive juices (hydrochloric acid) reduce their efficiency to break down and convert our food. In fact by the time we are 40 years of age they are 1000 times less acidic than a child under 5 years of age. There are however some simple natural enzymes that can help to digest your food.

Simple Digestive Aids:
Basil
The word Basil is derived from the Greek word for king. The ancient healers held it high regard for its abdominal healing powers.

Possible Benefits:
- Aids digestion
- Relieves gas and flatulence
- Reduces stomach cramps and nausea
- Promotes normal bowel function

How To Use It: Mix 1 teaspoon of dried basil herbs in _ cup of warm water. Steep for several minutes. Strain and drink 1 or 2 cups as needed daily.

Cayenne Pepper
Possible Benefits:
- Digestive Aid
- Stimulates the appetite and gastric juices.
- Reduces gas and flatulence.
- Relieves pain and inflammation.
- Improves metabolism
- Cayenne is very nutritious-high in vitamin C, B complex, Iron and Calcium.
- Beneficial on blood fats reducing triglycerides and LDL (bad) Cholesterol.
- Helps break down blood clots efficiently

How To Use It: One capsule can be take before each meal. Take up to 3 capsules daily.

Refer to section on 'Superfoods' for information on:
Apple Cider Vinegar and Beetroot

Fluid Intake – Your fluid intake is very important. As an average you should be consuming between 45ml of fluid per day for every kilogram of body weight. For an individual weighing 63 kg (10 stone) they should be drinking no less than 2 _ litres of fluid per day, especially if unwell. Fluids and in particular clean water help maintain a healthy body function and assist the kidneys in cleansing the body. A simple sign of being dehydrated is that your urine will be a darker colour than normal. The colour of urine should be very nearly clear. Drinking clean water with no additives including carbonate can also help with removing water that has seeped into the wrong part of the body (effusates). This will also assist with weight reduction and improved health.

Evacuation of Waste – Constipation. Do not under estimate the importance of evacuating wastes from the body. If you are suffering from constipation then there is a likelihood that you are reintroducing the toxins back into your body. If this situation continues for any length of time you will become extremely ill and if suffering with a chronic illness you will not be able to restore yourself to normal health. It is not infrequent for patients on chemotherapy to suffer with constipation. If you have not had a bowel movement during any 24 hours period take a laxative just to be on the safe side. Flaxseed Flake and Whole Flaxseed in particular are extremely beneficial in preventing constipation and aiding the colon, the intestines and digestive tract.

How's this for an example of the importance of a regular bowel!
I had been travelling abroad for 5 days and had not bothered to take a supply of Flaxseed Flake with me and at the same time ran out of Flaxseed Oil whilst on my travels. On my return I was prescribed Warfarin as a precaution from thrombosis and at exactly the same time I started a new cycle of chemotherapy. Not realising it, but I had not had a bowel movement for more than 24 hours. I became very unwell during the night and was admitted to A&E, discharged, only to return within 12 hours with a life threatening condition. I had toxins from the bowel back up to both

my kidney and liver. But once back on the flax seed oil and whole flax seed I returned to good health – and I always make sure the bowels are working well now!

Why Our Body's Need Fat!

To sustain good health or repair a damaged body there are three food elements that **MUST** be in balance as part of our diet. These three fundamental basic elements of nutrition are:
Carbohydrates, Proteins and Fats.
The basic nutrient 'fat' is essential for life. Dr Johanna Budwig identified it as centrally significant for almost every vital function of the body. She made comparisons with other important nutrients and stated quite categorically that fat in the correct proportions contains by far the greatest force of energy that the body can access immediately.

Fat – The Life Giving Principles
Dr Budwig identified in her research a wealth of electrons in 'good' fats such as those found in Flaxseed oil. These good fats will assist naturally the body to heal and restore anyone suffering with:
- Arrest and Angina
- Arteriosclerosis, Arthritis.
- Allergies, Acne, Eczema, Psoriasis and Dry Skin
- Viral Infection
- Cancer Prevention, Treatment and Tumour Formation.
- Diabetes, Regulation of Blood Sugar and of Insulin.
- Fatigue and Depression
- Fatty Liver and Irregular Gall Bladder Functions
- Fungal and Bacterial Infections
- High Cholesterol Levels.
- High Blood Pressure
- Kidney Disease.
- Multiple Sclerosis
- Rheumatism
- Strokes and Heart Attacks, Heart Infarction

Body Metabolism, Synthesis and Functions - Dependent Upon EFA's: The body requires essential fatty acids for the body to function properly. The following list is only a small part of what EFA's may assist with.

- Hormonal synthesis and stimulation of steroid production
- Endocrine hormones directed to their target cells
- Mediates and balancing of the immune response
- Regulates the response to pain and inflammation
- Regulates pressure in the eye
- Regulates bodily secretions
- Aids the control of blood vessels
- Regulates smooth muscle reflexes
- Regulates cellular division (mitosis)
- Regulates essential materials through the cellular wall
- Aids in the transportation of oxygen to the bodily tissues via the red blood cells
- Aids regulation of kidney function and fluid balance
- Aids in synthesizing and metabolising saturated fats and keeping them fluid in the blood stream
- Prevents excess clumping of blood cells, a major cause of stroke
- Aids in preventing the formation of plaque within coronary arteries
- A major energy source for the heart muscle

Other Beneficial Fatty Acid Oils

There are also other plant-derived oils that are being used for enhancing health issues. Evening primrose, black currant and borage oils all contain gamma-linolenic acid, an Omega-6 fatty acid. These oils are beneficial and very popular, but the amount of research on GLA supplements is not as well founded or documented as that of Omega 3 (ALA) oils. This is mainly due to GLA being able to be formed from linoleic acid (Omega-6) by synthesis within our body's own metabolic process. However, most natural sources of GLA are much richer in linoleic acid than

GLA. For example, evening primrose contains only 9% GLA, but contains 72% linoleic acid. Black currant although high in GLA it also contains a GLA inhibitor.

In most instances, oils that are high linoleic acid such as safflower (78%) sunflower (69%) and soya (61%) oil may provide the parent omega fatty acid for the to synthesise into Gla at a relatively modest cost, but these are exceptionally high in omega-6, something we definitely do not need any addition to our diet. In particular with diabetics, GLA supplementation has been shown to improve nerve function, which would aid diabetics in preventing in preventing nerve disease.

Robert Erdmann, Ph.D in his book 'Fats That Can Save Your Life' relates a case where an individual suffering with a painfully discomforting whip-lash injury improves the probable nerve damage with GLA supplementation. If you are considering a supplement of GLA then a daily dose of Borage Oil is likely the best source with 39% GLA.

Are You Getting Your Money's Worth?

Many research papers and findings indicate the benefits that can be found in taking Omega-3 that is associated with fish oils and the presence of eicosapentaenoic acid (EPA). EPA is however synthesised in the body from the parent alpha-omega oil (ALA) alpha-linolenic acid, the essential fatty acid in flaxseed oil. But to achieve this conversion and synthesis in the body, saturated fats should be reduced.

Flaxseed oil contains up to twice the amount of Omega-3 oil when compared to fish oils and is also a good source for linoleic acid as well.

Although EPA (from Cod Liver Oil) and GLA (Evening Primrose) supplements have been shown to be very beneficial in the treatment of many health conditions, the actual dosages required to produce the therapeutic desired effect are quite high, and very often cost prohibitive to achieve the same level of result as flaxseed oil.

Flaxseed oil is the best choice as an Omega-3 supplement. Not only is it mother nature's richest source of Omaega-3 it also has significant nutritional benefits over fish related oils, as well as being the best choice economically.

It is very important to ensure that you are receiving the correct level of dose of omega-3, to take less than the desired amount may not bring any benefit.

As an example for the treatment of rheumatoid arthritis, research and studies have indicated impressively positive results with GLA and EPA dosages of 1.4 grams and 1.8 grams, respectively. But, supplementing with less than the effective dose is not likely to produce the same beneficial improvement.

The dosage level of supplementation to achieve a therapeutic improvement is quite low with both flaxseed oil and borage oil due to them having very high levels of ALA and GLA respectively and the cost is likely to less than half of any other source.

Lignans And SDG - An Additional Benefit

Flaxseeds are the most abundant source of lignans and a very special lignan compound known as SDG. The existence of SDG has been known of for some decades but recent research has indicated that this component of flaxseed may pose significant benefits in certain cancer diseases.

Researchers and scientists at (SRC) together with the University of Saskatchewan, Department of Physiology and the University of Western Ontario, London Health Sciences Centre have now developed the technology to extract the valuable SDG from the defatted flaxseed. That's another reason why either whole ground flax seed or defatted flax flake is so important within our diet. Patent applications for extracting SDG from defatted flaxseed meal have been applied for in both Canada and Finland.

However, Brown flaxseed from Canada has up to 3% SDG (secoisolariciresinol diglucoside) and is only found in either the whole seed or the defatted flake.

SDG is a phytochemical that occurs naturally in whole flax seed which has demonstrated remarkable positive health benefits in fighting cancer, lupus nephritis, diabetes and atherosclerosis.

SDG and plant lignans are known to aid in relieving menopausal hot flashes, as well as an effective anticancer, antifungal and antiviral activity. Maybe the most significant of the actions of SDG and lignans is the anticancer/anti-tumoural effects that I can personally attest to.

A significant amount of research has shown that the lignans from flaxseed have a tremendous benefit to our well-being and they are synthesised and changed by our intestinal bacteria to elementary compounds that are extremely proactive in protecting against cancer, in particular breast and colon cancers.

Some oil manufacturers believe a high lignan flaxseed oil may have some benefits for women going through menopause or women at risk for breast cancer. However, research by Professor Lillian Thompson has indicated a possible benefit in this respect with freshly ground flaxseed as this contains a much higher proportion of the important lignan SDG.

But in my opinion I believe that supplementing with two heaped tablespoons of fresh ground flaxseed and between 1 to 2 tablespoons of flaxseed oil will give the greatest protection and benefit.

It is currently estimated that as many as one in six women will develop breast cancer in their lifetime.

How To Buy Flaxseed Oil

Consumers must be aware that because flax seed oil is a super-polyunsaturated oil, it is extremely susceptible to damage by heat, light and oxygen. Once the oil is damaged, it is a rich source of toxic molecules known as lipid peroxides. These molecules can actually do the body harm and should not be ingested.

Lipid peroxides are associated with an extremely bitter or fishy type taste and rancidity. The best way of identifying if flaxseed oil is rancid, is by taste. The slightly unpleasant fish type taste or bitterness is a close approximation of the level of lipid peroxides.

Until Stone Mills began pressing organic oils to the standards that would be acceptable to Dr Budwig, most if not all the flax seed oil being sold in the UK was pressed and imported from the West Coast of the USA.

Manufacturers do their best to ensure that their product reaches the customer in good condition, but unfortunately delays in delivery, warehousing or customs inspection may result in an inferior product reaching the customer.

When buying flaxseed oil it although it may kept at an ambient temperature of around 15•C although it is best to purchase oil that has been refrigerated during storage.

The oil I can recommend is Stone Mills Organic Oils a cold expeller pressing company who supply lignan rich flaxseed oil throughout Europe as well as defatted flaxseed flake and whole flaxseed. They have daily deliveries direct to their merchants and stores, or it can be bought from them within 24 hours of having been pressed by direct mail order.

When Your Told It's Cancer

I began to write this section following an enquiry by one of Oliver's Angels – Carmel his secretary. Discussing some of the benefits of flax seed oil with Carmel she asked something that most other family, friends or acquaintances had been too frightened to ask, probably because I used to make jokes about my underlying illness.

"What is it like to be told you've only a couple of months to live".
"Numb" I replied, "But only for the first day, I knew I had to get to work to cure myself".

That is exactly where it is at.

Do not shove it under the carpet, hide it within your emotions, you must understand that the word cancer is not a death sentence, in many instances it is only a rather inconvenient illness.

You must get hold of both your conscious state of mind and your sub-conscious state and tell yourself that YOU WILL GET CURED, with or without conventional medicine, with or without complimentary or alternative medicine (CAM).

True being told you have cancer is nothing less than devastating. My comments are not meant to be flippant, they are meant to get you on the right track, both in your mind and your body.

Being informed by someone who has never suffered with the illness does not make it any easier, believe it not I think many oncologists are just as frightened in telling you the diagnosis and prognosis as you are in hearing it. They do not know what the feeling is. I've been told by acquaintances who have been diagnosed with cancer that well meaning oncologists have used remarks such as "Don't worry"…Er…are they on the same planet as us…how can you not worry. You worry for your partner, your family, your children, your friends and yourself.

But I will say it…DON'T WORRY 'cause I have been through the grey days (did not have any black days), the days when you're not so sure about yourself, your not so certain on what road to take, the isolation of feeling alone. Remember our mind is the key as well as the nutrition in surviving cancer and many other chronic illnesses.

Your immune system and its responses are controlled by the brain, so you need to be in a positive not a negative thought process.

In my opinion as humble as it is, I believe with the right tools, state of mind and determination, that cancer (that word again), is probably easier to deal with and possible to beat than heart infarction, diabetes or osteoporosis.

One of the most important benefits I found from changing my diet was that with the flax seed oil - it gave me the calmness needed to deal with the illness and I was not the most patient person in the world!

How Did I Deal With The Actual Illness

After reading many research papers, books and case studies I came to the conclusion that cancer is two illnesses, but closely linked.

Firstly there is the primary tumour/tumours themselves and secondly, there is the mutagen effect from a dysfunctional immune system causing secondary metastasis. Some eminent oncologists believe that many cancers may be as a result of 15 or 20 years of systemic dysfunction due to nutritional deficiency, stress or toxins .

From the papers that I had read I believed my first approach was to remove the possible mutagens and also any inhibitors to the immune system. Once I had removed possible inhibitors, I then needed to optimise my immune system. Using flax seed oil, whole ground flax seed and a clean natural nutritious diet - I was then ready to fight the illness.

It worked. Firstly by removing possible mutagens I began to feel much better which is an encouragement to continue. Then by eventually perfecting my cooking techniques and eating habits I began to regain my health. Blood samples began to improve significantly. Life had now become very much easier.

So the up shot is, tell yourself you are dealing with two separate illnesses and each one can be beaten.

Another trick I used was to sit in a comfortable chair, close my eyes and imagine that my body's Natural Killer (NK) cells were zapping the cancer cells. I also pictured in my mind the Omega-3 from the flax seed oil flowing through my veins into every vital organ and repairing the tissues on the way. It really is beneficial if you believe what you are doing is working.

I've Lost My Appetite
Your appetite is one of the most important aspects in recovering from any chronic illness. Without good nourishment your body cannot thrive and survive. There are some tricks you can play which helps in regaining some of your pleasure in eating.

On page 56 I list some simple natural sources for aiding digestion and creating an appetite.

If you are on the Omega-3-Protein Diet you will find that flaxseed satiates the appetite giving you a full sensation. This is believed to be due to the way flax seed works within the digestive system whereby it allows food to remain longer and thus get processed into valuable enzymes for our body by our digestive juices.

It is best to eat little and often dividing your daily meals into four meals a day and following each meal you should consume the amount of flax seed oil and flax seed flake that is required under your programme.

If after trying the natural digestive remedies and you still are not eating properly I would recommend juicing all of your fruits and vegetables that form part of your diet. This allows the flesh and the bulk of the fruit or vegetable to be removed but still allows for the ingestion of all the good nutrients, vitamins and minerals. This is a superb way of enhancing your immune system even for those individuals who are not unwell.

Nutrition and Cancer Conference

European Conference on Nutrition and Cancer in Lyon, France June 22, 2001

One Third of Cancers Linked to Diet

Almost **one in three cancers could be prevented** through healthier eating, a major international conference heard this week. The European Prospective Investigation into Cancer and Nutrition (EPIC) is one of one of the world's largest studies investigating the relationship between the disease and what people eat. The study has confirmed many previous studies showing that **some food can increase the risks of cancer** while others can have a protective effect on the human body.
However, it has also provided some new ideas and raised doubts about previously long-held theories.
The study, which is looking at the diets of more than 500,000 people from nine European countries, has confirmed once again that **eating fruit and vegetables can ward off the disease,** in particular colon and rectal cancer.
However, curiously the study found no evidence to suggest they can ward off cancers of the stomach and lungs.
The preliminary results have also raised questions about the long-held belief that eating red meat can increase the risk of cancer.
For years many have been fearful that red meat, particularly beef, lamb and pork, could increase the risk of colorectal cancer. The study looked very closely at this issue and the results don't support that.
The study is looking into the different types of meat and why processed meat may be a greater risk than fresh meat and to see what is in processed meat that may increase the risks.
The study found that **excessive smoking and drinking** combined can **increase cancer risks by 50 times.** No surprise here. One researcher acknowledged that the findings could prove confusing for patients who want to change their diet to protect against

cancer. The study, which is ongoing, is not due to finish until at least 2003. But the research team is planning to publish a scientific paper examining the links between cancer and food in 2002.

CT Scans The Author's Liver

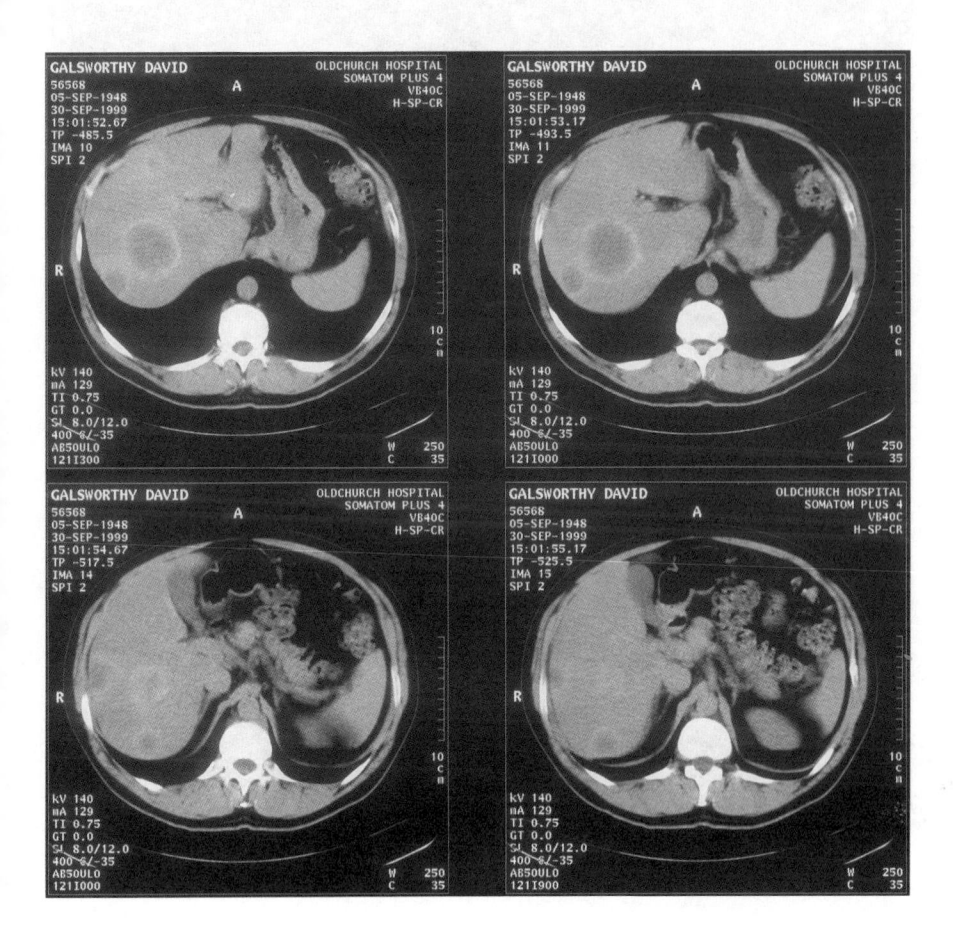

Scan 1: 30th September 1999, 7 weeks following initial diagnosis of cancer.

The liver was the primary organ that I concentrated on trying to repair. The top two scans clearly show a 4 cm diameter tumour in the middle of the liver. The lower two scans are at a different cross section of the liver.

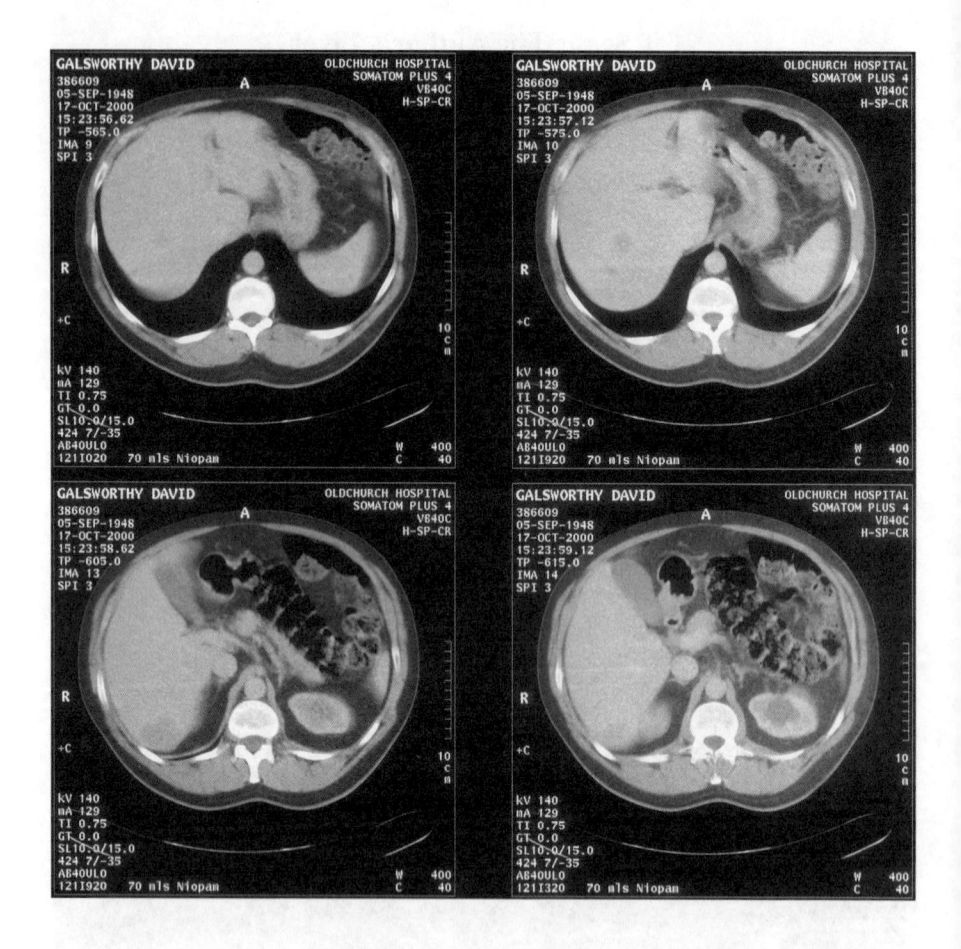

Scan 2: 17th October 2000.
12 months following the original scans on previous page, the 4 cm tumour has almost gone. Further CT scans in March 2001 would reveal an even greater improvement of the liver and other soft tissue tumours.

It is vitally important to protect the liver. Eating foods that put little strain on the liver is important. Reducing or removing toxic elements is of paramount importance.

The Body's Cleansing Organs

The Liver

The liver is the largest internal multi-functional organ in our body located under the dome of the diaphragm on the right hand side. The liver is divided into four lobes with the right lobe being the largest. The liver produces a fluid known as bile. Few of us appreciate the importance of the liver.
The main functions of the liver are:
The removal of toxins from the blood.
Aids in breaking down and digesting fats as well as aiding in the digestion of food.
The conversion of saturated fats to unsaturated fats when the body requires fat for energy.
The manufacture of Heparin, for the prevention of blood clotting.
The manufacture of blood proteins and blood clotting agents
The formation of antibodies.
The storage of vitamins A, D and B.
The storage of Glycogen a form of sugar.
The production of Fibrogen
The production of Albumin, which is a blood plasma protein.
An important component of all cell membranes.
A precursor for many hormones.
The breaking down and recycling of the iron-rich, oxygen saturated haemoglobin.
The removal of urea from amino acids and there dismantling of excess amino acids.
The liver syntheses good HDL cholesterol.

The traditional feeling of good spirits and well being is directly related to a healthy liver. In Chinese medicine and according to the Nei Ching " The liver has the functions of a military leader who excels in his strategic planning". It is also known to house the soul and therefore the deeper consciousness of oneself.
KEEP YOUR LIVER HEALTHY AND IT WILL REPAY YOU WITH VITALITY AND GOOD HEALTH

The Lungs
We are air-breathing vertebrates with two large respiratory organs known as the lungs, these lungs are our primary breathing mechanism. They are situated within the cavity of the chest and are responsible for aerating the blood with oxygen.
How do we breathe?
Air is drawn via the nasal track or mouth into the lungs when the muscles between the chest and the abdomen and the intercostals muscles contract, expanding the chest cavity and lowering the pressure between the lungs and chest wall as well as within the lungs. Each lung is covered with a thin membrane sac and both are connected to the windpipe known as the trachea by the air passageway the bronchus, and also to the heart by the pulmonary arteries.
The lungs are soft spongy and elasticised organs.
Each lung is divided into lobes separated by tissue. The right lung has three major lobes, whereas the left lung, which is slightly smaller, has two lobes. It does not finish there each lobe then sub divides into hundreds of lobules each with its own thin wall. Each lobule contains a bronchiole and clusters of very small sacs called alveoli.
Inside the lungs and about two thirds of the way up from the base is the helum which is the point at which the pulmonary, bronchial arteries, veins and lymphatic vessels enter the lungs.
On entering the lung the main bronchus divides into what is known as the bronchi and then subdivisions into many branches and when viewed has the appearance of an inverted tree. Branches within the lung with diameters less than 3 mm are known as bronchioles, which lead to the alveoli, this is where the gas molecules of oxygen and carbon dioxide are exchanged between the respiratory voids and the blood capillaries.
As well as respiratory activities, the lungs perform other body functions. They are able to absorb and excrete alcohol and water. The lungs normally excrete about 1 litre of water daily. Fats in the bloodstream (lipids) are removed and stored in the alveodor cells. The lung can store animal starch (glycogen) and metabolise it for

use by the body. This metabolisation is an aid to the liver in the regulation of starches (carbohydrates).

The Kidneys

As humans we have two kidneys. Both kidneys rest against the rear muscles in the upper abdomen and are located beneath the dome of the diaphragm and are further protected by the ribs.
Our kidneys have several main functions:
- Excretion of wastes - mainly consisting of urea and salts from blood plasma, including water soluble toxic substances and drugs.
- Regulation and maintenance of water and electrolyte content of the body. This endocrine (secretion to the blood) function allows us to eat and drink as to our tastes and habit without the need for changing the composition of the fluid compartments.
- Maintaining the body's acid - base balance (pH).
- Retention of vital proteins and glucose

Each kidney has 1 million minute-coiled tubes known as nephrons and these make up the basic functioning units of the kidney. These nephron filters prepare for the break down of waste material as well as the reusable material and water from the blood. Much of the water is reusable along with useful material, which is secreted and reabsorbed by the blood. What material the kidney does not put back into the body goes as waste, which passes down and along the ureters to the bladder.

The kidneys filter about up to 40-50 litres of blood per minute.

The kidneys (renal) supply of blood is approximately twenty percent of the output of the cardiovascular system, the heart.

The kidneys play an important part in regulating the water content in the body and aids in keeping the body's temperature under control. The kidneys are also associated with the adrenal glands, bones, bone marrow, brain and parathyroid. A general lack of energy can indicate an imbalance of the kidneys

Mad As A Hatter - Is Dental Amalgam Safe?

'Mad as a hatter'. This description of milliners of the 19th century came about due to the use of mercury in their trade of making hats. Frequently after many years and continual use of mercury they were carted off to the asylum 'As Mad As A Hatter'.

The debate and controversy over amalgam dental fillings has gone on for 150 years, and that position still remains the same today. The dental industries professional bodies unanimously maintain that there is no scientific evidence to prove that the use of mercury in 'silver fillings' is toxic to the body.
("The absence of evidence is not evidence of absence". – *Carl Sagan*).
However, the antagonists say that they are armed with scientific evidence that supports their view, that mercury does cause toxicity to vital organs of the body including the kidneys, gastro-intestinal tract and the nervous system. Some reports say that mercury can be transferred/transmitted via the nervous system and cause problems to the brain.
To give my case history:
In trying to find a cure for my illness it was suggested that I consider heavy metal (mercury in particular) toxicity with reference to my kidneys and liver, both of which I was having problems with. I visited my dentist of 25 years (his name and practice are immaterial) and asked if there was a possibility of heavy metal poisoning from amalgam fillings, his comment "Where did you ever get such an idea from". Not content with such an off the cuff remark I visited another dental practice of Marc Mortiboys who inspected my existing amalgam fillings. On the first visit Dr Mortiboys recognised that I may have an amalgam toxicity problem and referred me to Professor David Schweitzer for specialist tests to ascertain the extent of the problem. Professor Schweitzer's examination and tests, both blood and urine, showed that I had a level of 10 ppm (ten parts per million) of mercury in my urine, a very high level of toxicity that was as a result of amalgam dental fillings. I went back to Dr

Mortiboys for the specialist removal and replacement of all amalgam fillings. Some month's later further tests by Professor Schweitzer showed a level of 1 ppm (one part per million) of mercury in my urine. Independently, further blood tests conducted by Professor Oliver after 2 months of the dental treatment revealed that my creatinine level (a measure of kidney function) had returned to normal.

No doubt the debate and the fighting will carry on. My position is that I would never have another tooth cavity filled with amalgam filling again, nor would any of my family, as there are plenty of other alternative mediums available to the dentist.

But, the decision is yours – Do you want to end up as mad as a hatter?

Cancer of the Large Bowel (Colon and Rectum)
What is cancer?
Cancer is not a single disease, nor does it have a single cause, nor a single form of treatment. At the last count there was more than 200 different forms of cancer, each individual with its own name and treatment protocol.

The tissue and organs of our body's consist of minute building blocks known as cells. Cancer is a disease whereby the cells have grown out of control. We have a multitude of different cells in our body, liver cells specifically do the work in the liver, pancreatic cells work in the pancreas and so on. But all cells have a metabolic process whereby they multiply naturally repairing and reproducing themselves mostly by a similar process. When our body is fit and well, this division of cells (respiration) takes place in a controlled predetermined manner.

If however, the process begins to get out of control, and the body's immune response is deficient in some way, the cells will continue to divide which may develop into a into a lump which is called a tumour.

Tumours can be either malignant or benign.

With a benign tumour the cells remain where the lump has been formed and do not spread to other parts of the body and as such are referred to as non-cancerous.

If the lump continues to grow at the original site this may give rise to problems where the lump (tumour) can cause pressure on surrounding organ.

With a cancerous or malignant tumour the malignant cells of the lump have the ability to spread from the original site to other vital organs or tissue. Any cancerous tumour, if left untreated is likely to invade adjoining or surrounding tissue. When cancerous cells travel away from the original site or primary site they travel in the blood stream and the lymphatic system, very often forming new tumours, again with the cells dividing out of control at the new site. These new sites are referred to as secondary tumours or a metastasis. For a doctor to ascertain if a tumour is cancerous or not, they will remove a sample of the tumour tissue and under a microscope the tissue is examined – this is known as a biopsy.

The Large Bowel (colon and rectum)
The bowel is divided in two parts, the small bowel and the large bowel both form part of our digestive system. The large bowel consists of the rectum and colon.
When we consume our food, it travels down the gullet (oesophagus) to the stomach, where our digestion system starts to get to work. The food then travels down through the small bowel, where nutrients are synthesised and taken into our body. The food that has been digested then enters the large bowel where water is absorbed by the colon.
The remaining waste material known as stools or faeces, is held in the back passage or rectum until it is ready to be passed from the body through the anus as a bowel movement (motion). The colon and rectum will hold up to 5 bowel movements at any one time and it extremely important that these are excreted regularly. As a guide, if you consume 3 meals a day then you should be removing the waste with bowel movements 3 times a day. The waste products from the food we eat may take anything from 18 hours to 30 hours to pass through our bodies. A regular diet containing fibre and fresh whole ground flaxseed will aid bowel movements by retaining water for lubricating the faeces travel and exit.
It is more frequent for cancer to develop in the large bowel.
It is not uncommon for some people with cancer of the bowel to need to have a colostomy although the percentage is relatively low. Many hospitals have specially trained nurses called stoma care nurses who will usually meet you before an operation and discuss the procedures and what is involved. More information is available from the British Colostomy Association, details at the rear of the book.

Bowel Cancer Surgery
The specialist surgeon or a member of his team will discuss the most appropriate type of surgery, depending on the stage of the cancer. Surgical removal of the tumour is the most common form of treating cancer of the large bowel. Chemotherapy is often given, sometimes before and sometimes after the surgery.
Having removed the tumour the surgeon takes the two open ends of the bowel and then joins them together again. Any lymph nodes near to the bowel are also removed and sent away for a biopsy to ascertain if the cancer has spread, it is not uncommon for it to affect the lymph system. If the bowel cannot be rejoined, it can be repositioned in the abdominal cavity and brought out onto the skin of the abdominal wall. This procedure is referred to as a colostomy and the open end of the bowel is a stoma. The stoma is then covered by a bag to collect the stool or bowel movements.
The number of people suffering with cancer of the large bowel that require a colostomy bag is quite small.

Symptoms of Cancer of the Large Bowel
Cancer of the large bowel may include any of the following:
- A feeling of not having emptied your bowel after a bowel movement
- For no obvious reason-frequent diarrhoea or constipation
- Blood in the stool or very dark/black stools
- Weight loss
- Unexpected pain in the abdomen or back passage

Cancer of the large bowel may result in a blockage or obstruction within the bowel. The symptoms of this are bloated/full sensation of the abdomen, constipation, griping pain or sickness.
Always seek attention from your GP or doctor if you have suffered with any of the above symptoms.

A naming system for cancer staging has been devised as follows:
Staging:
Dukes A - Cancer is within the bowel wall.
Dukes B - Cancer has spread through the bowel wall, but the lymph nodes are not affected.
Dukes C - Cancer has spread to one or more of the lymph nodes nearby.
Dukes D - the cancer has spread to another part of the body (secondary cancer).
Research on Nutritional Prevention
One of the world's foremost authorities on nutrition, flaxseed, flaxseed oil and cancer is Professor Lillian Thompson of the Department of Nutritional Science at Toronto University, Canada. Professor Thompson and her team have found that plant lignans and especially a lignan known as SDG which is only found in whole ground flaxseed significantly reduced the proliferation of four types of human colon tumour cell lines, even though they were incubated with several levels of cancer promoters. Much of the credit for the anti-tumoural activity may well be due to SDG. SDG is covered later in more detail.
Much of the data on colon cancer and nutritional diets are covered in the following section on breast cancer.
The Omega-3 Protein Diet can be found on page 87.

A Miracle, A Case Study
Marion had heard of my health improvements from my sister Irene. Like many other individuals and myself if you have been diagnosed with cancer you tend to cling onto every hope and many investigate all sorts of possible 'cures'. Marion visited me with her husband Jim and I explained the diet I had used. I impressed on Marion that the diet was purely natural nutrition and an important part of the diet was the removal of immune system inhibitors such as preservatives in food and hydrogenated oils from processed food. By combining good balanced nutrition there was a chance of a much improve quality of life. Marion began taking the flaxseed oil about 5 days prior to her first course of

chemotherapy. Marion was about to start a new chemotherapy drug where the side effects were not very pleasant, the previous chemotherapy regime had not improved her health situation and she had a large tumour completely encircling her colon. Three weeks after the start on this new chemo course she had another cycle of chemo administered, but she was quite unwell following this second cycle. I visited Marion on the Sunday, 4 days following this second cycle. Unfortunately I did not get to see her as an ambulance was taking her to hospital as an emergency admission. Marion spent something in the region of 8 weeks in hospital, 2 weeks in Chelmsford Hospital and six weeks back at Southend Hospital and a period in intensive care. During this time Marion underwent major surgery to investigate the blockage of the colon. The surgeon related his findings later to Marion by informing her that having opened up the abdomen, investigating the colon, he was unable to find any tumour, but he did find a small opening in the colon wall where the tumour had been present.

From what both Marion and Jim had been told after the surgery, was the tumour had grown through the colon wall and had probably caused a blockage of the colon. This blockage had caused a build up of waste in Marion's body. With the tumour now gone the colon seeped waste material into surrounding tissue and the blood stream, which caused the onset of peritonitis (blood poisoning).

After this ordeal Marion was convinced that by taking flaxseed oil and flaxseed she had saved her life. On leaving hospital her body weight had reduced substantially to a little over 6 stone. Starting back on the Omega-3 Protein Diet she found that for the first two weeks her weight increased daily by _ kg (1 pound). Several weeks later she feels her health and well-being is improving each day and her weight has steadied to about 1kg increase each week.

Marion is one determined lady, she believed in nutrition as a possible benefit to health and the likely eradication of chronic illness or disease. I wish Marion and Jim good health.

Breast Cancer - Prevented Naturally!

Breast cancer, is every woman's, dread and fear and quite rightly so.

Jade Beutler the author of Understanding Fats and Oils, Your Guide to Healing with EFA's and Flax For Life describes the threat of the illness in woman as a national health tragedy.

There has been some excellent progress with some chemotherapy regimes, but noting some of the side effects, they appear to be alarmingly totally unnecessary.

The recent estimates suggest that in assessing the risks of contracting breast cancer vary from about one in eight to one in six women who it is thought will during their lifetime become afflicted with this potentially disfiguring and sometimes fatal disease.

Unfortunately the medical profession do not appear to have got the message to the general public that any woman irrespective of family history are at risk. This ambivalence by the medical profession has fostered a misconception among the fairer sex, that, if they do not have a family history of breast cancer, they are at a low risk.

This misconception, misinformation by those charged with our health issues is totally to the contrary of new studies and newly diagnosed cases of breast cancer in women with no known family history of the illness.

Every woman from her mid teens should regularly complete a self-examination of her breasts.

Literature and leaflets on how to go about the examination and what to look for are available from your doctor and most out-patients departments at your local hospital.

Self examination is absolutely essential if any problems are to be dealt with at an early stage. A regular mammography is important in identifying and detecting the presence of a lump, although there are new 'non-invasive devices' that are excellent for the woman who would like a screening more often than that recommended by the local health authorities.

For many of the common cancers, there is now growing evidence and acceptance that these cancers may develop as a result of a life times accumulation of small quantities of un-repaired DNA damage.
'A Mission – The Orchid Cancer Appeal'.

Early detection and improving resistance by optimising the immune system are extremely important in either defeating the illness or preventing it in the first place. It is important therefore to take an aggressive preventative approach, and that approach almost certainly should include both freshly whole ground flaxseed and flaxseed oil.
One eminent Complimentary and Alternative (CAM) practitioner and academic Professor David Schweitzer, one of the world's leading Humoral Pathologists says that he is able to detect cancer four to five years before regular conventional screening, X-Ray or imaging diagnosis. Professor Schweitzer says that cancer may be present for as long as five years, undetectable by X-ray, although new detection methods may identify 'hot spots' using non-invasive thermal imaging, these methods are proving extremely useful as a diagnostic tool.

The most standard medical treatment for diagnosed breast cancer would include a lumpectomy, which is the part removal of the breast and lump. Or, another method is known as a mastectomy, which is the total removal of the breast and what often accompanies both is chemotherapy and or radiation.
Very often this type of treatment is effective in ameliorating the tumour and occasionally the disease.
Unfortunately the result from such devastating procedures on the body by conventional medical practices is traumatic to the psyche of the patient and their overall well being and health.

The answer may well be a concerted effort to change some minor life style habits - diet.

Is This Natures Answer To Preventing Breast Cancer?
Some of the leading National Health Agencies and Charitable Health Organisations have been investigating nutrition, diet and nutritional supplementation as a likely answer in reducing the occurrence of breast cancer.

The (NCI) National Cancer Institute of America began focusing on nutrition and diet and the relevant dietary habits as long ago as 15 years and gave out grants accordingly. The objectives of the research were to ascertain the likelihood of a possible preventative method that may avoid contracting certain types of cancers.

An ongoing study due to finish in 2003 is EPIC (European Prospective Investigation into Cancer and Nutrition). The study is the largest ever conducted and involves 500,000 European nationals from 9 countries. Some of the preliminary findings are interesting. The study has shown that some foods can increase the risk of cancer, whilst a nutritious balanced diet may possibly reduce cancer by up to 30%. There has also been doubt cast on some long standing beliefs, one is that the eating of red meat may be attributable to a higher risk of cancer – the existing findings do not support that thinking. There will be a scientific paper published in 2002 examining the links between cancer and food.
European Conference on Nutrition and Cancer – Lyon 22nd June 2001

Many research organisation and academics have looked at a variety of fruits, vegetables and natural organic grains that may possess potent cancer fighting or anti-tumoural components known as phytochemicals and phytonutrients, these are naturally occurring, non-toxic plant chemicals.

As I mentioned earlier one of the most impressively powerful phytochemicals is SDG, which is known to have anti-tumoural activity. These naturally occurring plant phytonutrients once ingested are metabolised by the body and converted to elements that are in competition with oestrogen for binding sites on oestrogen receptors. The result is the removal of excess oestrogen, which has been linked to the incidence of breast and colon cancer. The excess oestrogen, which has been linked with colon and breast cancer is naturally removed from the body.

It is not only the possible cancer preventative effects of lignans, SDG and flax seed that is of the greatest interest, it is also the possible beneficial effects of flax seed when a cancer illness has been diagnosed, as I can attest to.

In the USA, a study of more than one hundred women revealed that woman with the highest breast tissue content of EFA/Omega-3 had the lowest incidence of breast cancer. As for the women in the study group that contracted breast cancer, the women with the greatest level of Omega-3 in surrounding breast tissue also had the lowest incidence of metastasis (tumours spreading from the original breast site to other vital organs).

The relevance of this study is that woman fighting breast cancer may prevent secondary metastasis with the ingestion of ground whole flaxseed rich in lignans and SDG and flaxseed oil enabling consumption of a concentrated form of Omega-3.

Lignans and SDG - An Anti-Tumour Aid

Whole flax seed, Defatted Flaxseed Flake possess the following benefits to health:
- Powerful Antioxidant
- Anti-Tumour,
- Anti- Bacterial,
- Anti-Viral
- Anti-Fungal
- Anti-Oestrogenic Ability
- Oestrogen Mimicking Effect - preventing the long term side effects associated with oestrogen therapy

Prevention – The First Line Of Defence

All women, regardless of their family history of breast cancer should consume one to two tablespoons of Lignan Rich Flax Seed Oil and two tablespoons of ground whole flaxseed or Defatted Flake a day as a major preventative measure against breast cancer disease.
The removal of hydrogenated oils and trans fats from the diet is important.
Don't forget to consume more fruit and vegetables.

References:
Thompson LU, et al.: Mammalian lignan production from various foods. Nutrition/Cancer 16:43- 52, 1991.
Serraino M and Thompson LU: Flaxseed supplementation and early markers of colon carcinogenesis. Cancer Letters 63:159-65, 1992.
Serraino M and Thompson LU: The effect of flaxseed on early risk markers for mammary carcinogenesis. Cancer Letters 60:135-42, 1991.
Dr Ross Pelton: Preventing Breast Cancer

Omega-3-Protein Diet - V For Victory Not Victim
Prohibited for the first 90 days
Anything that contains hydrogenated oil or fat, these include: Margarines, Spreads, Commercial Vegetable Oils, Salad Oils.
All processed foods that contain preservatives.
Non foods such as refined sugars, sweetened jams, confectionary, orange juice in cartons (squeeze your own).
From the bakers pastries and breads with refined flour or hydrogenated oils/fats
Pre-cooked meats, sausages and pates that contain preservatives.
Animal fats such as lard, dripping and beef suet.
Red meat.
Chocolate.
Refer to 'Super Foods' section for some guide lines on what will give you that edge.

THE FIRST DAY ONLY
Start First Day In The Morning- Repeat At Midday and 6pm
- 5 tablespoons (80ml) of Flaxseed Oil mixed with 1 (15ml) tablespoon of honey and 1 glass of Purple Grape Juice or a glass of Champagne.
- Champagne has a positive benefit within this diet as it is easily absorbed. A little water to quench the thirst may be taken during this first day.
- 1 Tablespoon Apple Cider Vinegar in glass of water

No Sugar: Purple Grape Juice or honey must be taken for sweetening in place of sugar
A Beverage 3 Times Per Day: 1 cup Peppermint, Rose Hip or Black or Green tea is allowed before midday. These may be sweetened to taste with honey.

THE DIET PLAN SHOULD CONTINUE EACH DAY AS FOLLOWS:

BEFORE BREAKFAST – These kick start the digestion with good intestinal bacteria. 150ml (1 glass) of either of the following:
- Buttermilk or Acidophilus Milk.
- 1 Tbsp of Apple Cider Vinegar in water (compulsory)

BREAKFAST – Breakfast should be light and wholesome. Fresh Fruit or Berries in Season, e.g. Blackberries, Cherries, Strawberries, Grated Apple. With a topping of Dessert Crème.
   Add 2 tablespoons of – Defatted Flax Flake or Ground Whole Flaxseed to either a separate drink of choosing or to the Dessert Crème topping on the fruit. These are an important part of the diet.
   Beverage of Herbal Tea, Black Tea or Fresh Juice.

Or, **The Quick Fix Breakfast:** In a liquidiser add 100ml of water, one apple or pear, a handful of strawberries. Add two tablespoons of pre-ground flax seed or flaxseed flake and three tablespoons of flaxseed oil and 6 tablespoons of Yoghurt or Quark. Liquidise into a 'Smoothy' vary the fruit to your choice – Tastes great and is bursting with nutrition.

MID MORNING TEA (10AM) –
150ml (wine glass) glass of pure fresh squeezed/juiced fruit juice

LUNCHEON

APPETISER
Small raw salad of choice - carrots, tomato, kohlrabi, grapes, celery or cauliflower. Horseradish, chives or parsley may be added for flavour. This may be as a salad on its own or combined as a wholemeal bread sandwich.
Before lunch take 1 tablespoon of Apple Cider Vinegar in a glass of water. This will aid digestion and is nutritionally beneficial

LUNCH – COOKED
Lunch can consist of home made chicken broth with vegetables and if available flaxseed bread. Add to broth, potatoes, barley, buckwheat, or millet. Superb nutritional value.
You may add flavour to the broth with mixed herbs.
Vary the type of vegetable, but always include some onion, tomato and carrot.
For a hearty meal, a baked jacket potato is always a favourite. By adding fresh chives, fresh parsley, caraway, or other herbs you will be increasing the nutritional value of your food. Only ever add parsley to a cooking dish in the last 5 minutes.

DESSERT – (compulsory)
Some fresh fruit or berries, try to vary from those used for breakfast. Add and cover fruit with Dessert Crème or consume crème separate. Vary the Dessert Crème (page 170) with vanilla or other flavouring

AFTERNOON (4PM) –
A small glass of organic red wine (no preservatives), purple grape juice or champagne with 1 heaped tablespoons of ground linseeds with honey to taste. Follow with (150ml) a glass of water.

EVENING MEAL/SUPPER –
This should be consumed no later than 7pm.
Supper may consist of:

Fish: Coldwater white fish such as cod, plaice, skate, halibut, sole or turbot. Avoid farmed reared salmon and trout.

Poultry: Chicken (without the skin), Rabbit, Turkey or Wild game dish. They should be grilled, baked or casseroled. Include a jacket potato, pasta or rice with steamed green vegetables.
Refer to recipe and meal suggestions.

Quick supper:
If you are in a hurry, an excellent nourishing supper is a homemade soup or broth with the chicken stock as the base. You may add Millet, Buckwheat or Oatmeal for extra nutrition.

Dessert:
A little fruit with a serving of Flax Dessert Crème refer p170.

Home Made Chicken Stock: You will need to consume at least one bowl of homemade chicken stock every day. Vary the taste with vegetables and flavouring.

Fluid Intake: It is important to have no less than 2 litre of fluid per day. Taking into account fruit juices you will still need to have 8 glasses of water spread throughout the day. Avoid fluids 30 minutes either side of a meal as this will reduce the efficiency of digestive juices.

Purple Grape Juice: This has several beneficial effects, try to locate a good quality and drink two glasses per day. Purple grape juice has shown to increase Nitric Oxide (NO) by 70% in the body as well as having high anti-oxidant properties. Nitric Oxide dilates the blood vessels and has shown benefits with blood circulation to the extremities.

Menopause and PMS - Is This Nature's Answer?

Some of the more enlightened menopausal women have found a simple trick to benefiting their health and that is to correctly balanced their intake of oils and fats. Many have discovered that by supplementing with omega-3 rich sources such as flaxseed oil and ground whole flax seed, they frequently find a reduction in bloating, breast tenderness, hot flushes, swelling, and other symptoms related to menopause and PMS.

Flaxseed oil and in particular Omega 3 are well documented for its calming effects on the brain. A benefit of this calming effect is a reduction in irritability allowing them to regain control of their lives. Numerous studies and research have confirmed that women find these benefits when supplementing with this unique 'intelligent' oil.

In every day life women have found great improvement in nail strength, an unexpected improvement in their skin texture and its appearance as well as soft shiny hair.

Research findings have also recently revealed that a women's menstrual cycle can also be regulated effectively with flaxseed oil or whole ground flax seed.

In one study, women consuming flaxseed oil did not miss a single cycle, in comparison to a control group that missed several.

It may be a little too early and still on the biochemists bench but Mother Nature may have given us lignans and Omega-3 as a natural aid in preventing some of the major biological effects of menopause and PMS related conditions.

One day the humble flaxseed may also replace the necessity for HRT in post-menopausal women due to the resemblance of lignans to oestrogen at the receptor site, but without the potential side effects and risks of oestrogen therapy.

Benefits Of Lignan Rich Flaxseed Oil And Flax Flake
- Prevention of Oestrogen Related Cancers
- Prevention of Metastasis of Cancerous Tumours
- Reduction in Hot Flashes and Irritability
- Induces calmness
- Reduction in Bloating and Breast Tenderness
- Regulation of Menstrual Cycle
- Improved Nail Strength
- Improvement in Skin Texture and Appearance
- Improvement in Hair Sheen and Appearance

Who's In Charge of Your Change

The Stone Mills formula for Essentially Mine™ has been developed specifically for woman of all ages. Women who may be beginning to experience some of the early signs of menopause or who have PMS symptoms will gain a tremendous benefit from this unique formula. Essentially Mine is likely to be of benefit to any woman from her mid teens and onwards.

All of us have been incorrectly programmed for decades in thinking that fat is bad. Sorry girls (and guys) go to the bottom of the class, we were all wrong!

Media advertising has brain washed us with attractive looking bodies on our TV's. Luscious hair blowing in the breeze and the perfect skin we all dream of. All of this is to sell more of their products.
Now lets pause a minute..........

Those attractive looking bodies are professional models that are paid an extremely large amount of money to look good. We'd all look good with that kind of expenditure. The beautiful flowing hair has just had one of the top hair stylists spend hours making sure it was right for the cameras, and that beautiful skin – its amazing what a little touch up here and a little touch up there can do.

Got the message!
Going back to us being incorrectly programmed about fats and that they are bad for us and they should be eliminated from our diet is completely wrong.... Why?

Fat-free cooking methods and foods are basically wrong, the intake of no-fat foods or those high in sugars and carbohydrates like breads, pastas, potatoes, rice cakes, and fat-free yoghurts are a recipe for disaster. If we start to conscientiously count up those fat grams we have to make sure we are counting the correct type of fats in our diet.
Many individuals have been eliminating all fats (even the healthy and essential ones), from their diets, these men and women will gain weight, succumb to depression and women will suffer pre-menopausal symptoms such as aggressiveness, mood swings, irritability, water retention, and breast tenderness, as well as dry skin, lack-lustre hair and brittle nails.
Many of these symptoms can be defeated if only the body was balanced correctly with the right oils and fats.

The fats in your diet MUST include Essential Fatty Acids such as Omega 3 not in tiny amounts from capsules but in good tablespoon servings.

By including these EFA's in your diet, adjusting and monitoring the other fats digested fats the omega 3 will work to remove from your body saturated fats, reduce adipose fats, control your weight, improve your skin, mind and health....

Just imagine all of these benefits –
                    What was that - a ssssmile!

What Does *'Essentially Mine™'* **Contain:**

There are some important ingredients in Essentially Mine. The major ingredients omega-3 and GLA help to balance the body fats and help to improve woman's lives.

Flax: Firstly there is cold expeller pressed flaxseed oil. Flax seed was chosen for its very high Omega-3 fatty acids content. The data and research on Omega 3 and essential fatty acids reaches epic proportions, mainly due to the incredible benefits that they have on the body. Flaxseed oil and its army of workers have been shown to relieve allergies, depression, fatigue, and it is a known aid and healing agent for topical conditions like eczema, psoriasis, acne, and dry skin.

Borage: Borage Oil contains nature's highest source of a very important EFA known as gamma-linolenic acid (GLA) from the Omega-6 fatty acid family. Many women swear by Evening Primrose, which is taken for its GLA content, but Borage oil has almost 3 fold the amount of GLA than Evening Primrose. The combination of Omega-3 from Flax seed oil and Omega-6 from Borage oil have proven beneficial results for their calming effects, reducing anxiety, controlling irritability, mood changes, headaches, and PMS along with other discomforts such as fluid retention and breast tenderness.

Rosemary: The herb rosemary is one of nature's wonder herbs. Earl Mindell in his book 'The New Herb Bible' describes rosemary as one of his hot 100's. Rosemary is well known as an antioxidant and has been used in oils to prevent rancidity, but there is research that suggests it is beneficial in relieving and alleviating migraines, it may reduce the risk of breast cancer and helps to preserve memory. A study at Penn State found that rats fed a diet supplemented with dried rosemary could protect them from carcinogens. Rosemary may also aid in combating cardiovascular issues, heart disease and control infections.

Now…you're the boss - take charge of your change.

Omega-3-Protein Diet - Let Your Diet Take The Strain
Avoid If Possible:
Anything that contains hydrogenated oil or fat, these include: Margarines, Spreads, Commercial Vegetable Oils, Salad Oils.
Processed Food that contain preservatives.
Non Foods such as refined sugars, jams, confectionary, orange juice in cartons (squeeze own).
Pastries and breads with refined flour or hydrogenated oils/fats from the bakers.
Pre-cooked meats, sausages and pates that contain preservatives.
In Moderation:
Animal fats such as lard, dripping and suet (fresh only).
Red meat and fresh meats should be organic or wild wherever possible.
Chocolate: only Belgium milk chocolate.
Dairy: Butter, Cheese.
Refer to 'Super Foods' section for some guide lines on what will give you that edge.

THE FIRST DAY ONLY
Start First Day In The Morning- Repeat At Midday and 6pm
- 5 tablespoons (80ml) of Flaxseed Oil mixed with 1 (15ml) tablespoon of honey and 1 glass of Purple Grape Juice
- 1 Tbsp Apple Cider Vinegar in glass of water

A little water to quench the thirst to be taken during this first day.
No Sugar: Purple Grape Juice or honey must be taken for sweetening in place of sugar (Not Diabetics).
A Beverage 3 Times Per Day: 1 cup Peppermint, Rose Hip or Black or Green tea is allowed before midday. These may be sweetened to taste with honey.

THE DIET PLAN SHOULD CONTINUE EACH DAY AS FOLLOWS:

BEFORE BREAKFAST – These kick start the digestion with good intestinal bacteria. 150ml (1 glass) of the following:
- Buttermilk, Acidophilus Milk or Kombucha Tea.
- 1 Tbsp Apple Cider Vinegar in glass of water (Compulsory)

BREAKFAST – Breakfast should be light and wholesome. Fresh Fruit or Berries in Season, e.g. Blackberries, Cherries, Strawberries, Grated Apple. With a topping of Dessert Crème.
Add 2 tablespoons of – Defatted Flax Flake or ground whole flaxseed to either a separate drink of choosing or to the Dessert Crème (p170) topping on the fruit. These are an important part of the diet.
Beverage of Herbal Tea, Black Tea or Fresh Juice.

Or, **The Quick Fix Breakfast:** In a liquidiser add 100ml of water, one cored and peeled apple or pear, a handful of strawberries. Add two tablespoons of pre-ground flax seed or flaxseed flake and two tablespoons of flaxseed oil and 4 tablespoons of Yoghurt or Quark. Liquidise into a 'Smoothey' vary the fruit to your choice – Taste's great and is bursting with nutrition.

MID MORNING TEA (10AM) –
150ml (wine glass) of pure fresh squeezed/juiced fruit juice

LUNCHEON
APPETISER
Small raw salad of choice - carrots, tomato, kohlrabi, grapes, celery or cauliflower. Horseradish, chives or parsley may be added for flavour. This may be as a salad on its own or combined as a wholemeal bread sandwich.
Before lunch take 1 tablespoon of Apple Cider Vinegar in a glass of water. This will aid digestion and is nutritionally beneficial

LUNCH

Lunch can consist of home made chicken broth with vegetables and if available flaxseed bread. Add to broth, potatoes, buckwheat, barley or millet. Superb nutritional value.
You may add flavour to the broth with mixed herbs.
Vary the type of vegetable, but always include some onion, tomato and carrot.
For a hearty meal, a baked jacket potato is always a favourite. By adding fresh chives, fresh parsley, caraway, or other herbs you will be increasing the nutritional value of your food. Only ever add parsley to a dish in the last 5 minutes of cooking.

DESSERT – (compulsory)

Some fresh fruit or berries, try to vary from those used for breakfast. Add and cover fruit with Dessert Crème or eat crème separate. Vary the flavour of Dessert Crème with vanilla or cinnamon.

AFTERNOON (4PM) –

A small glass of organic red wine (no preservatives), purple grape juice or champagne with 1 heaped tablespoons of ground linseeds with honey to taste. Follow with (150ml) a glass of water.

EVENING MEAL/SUPPER –

This should be consumed no later than 7pm. This may consist of:

Fish: Coldwater white fish such as cod, plaice, skate, halibut, sole or turbot – Grilled or Baked.
Avoid farmed reared salmon and trout.

Poultry: Chicken (without the skin), Rabbit, Turkey or wild game dish. These should be grilled or baked.
Refer to recipe and meal suggestions.

Beef or Lamb: Grilled or casseroled. (remove as much fat as possible). Include a jacket potato, pasta or rice with steamed green vegetables.

Quick supper:
An excellent nourishing supper is a homemade soup or broth with the chicken stock as the base. You may add Millet, Buckwheat or Oatmeal for extra nutrition.

Dessert:
A little fruit with a serving of Flax Dessert Crème (p170).

Fluid Intake: It is important to have no less than 2 litre of fluid per day. Taking into account fruit juices you will still need to have 8 glasses of water spread throughout the day. Avoid fluids 30 minutes either side of a meal as this will reduce the efficiency of digestive juices.

Purple Grape Juice: This has several beneficial effects, try to locate a good quality and drink two glasses per day. Purple grape juice has shown to increase Nitric Oxide (NO) by 70% in the body as well as having high anti-oxidant properties. Nitric Oxide dilates the blood vessels and has shown benefits with blood circulation to the extremities.

Weight Loss/Optimisation: Through the course of each day you are looking to consume no less than four tablespoons of flaxseed oil with a protein such as quark or yoghurt plus at least 3 tablespoons of ground whole flaxseed or flaxseed flake.
See chapter on weight.

For The Healthy: You will need to consume no less than two to four tablespoons of flaxseed oil each day plus two tablespoons of ground whole flaxseed

The 3P's - Preventing Prostate Problems
(3 P's A Night - Needs Attention)

The prostate is one of the most complicated and influential organs of the male body. A walnut-sized gland that surrounds the male urethra, its primary function is to produce an essential portion of the seminal fluid that carries sperm. In addition, the prostate also controls the outward flow of urine from the bladder. Due to this double role, signs of prostate problems can include both urinary and sexual difficulties.

There are two primary problems commonly experienced with the prostate. One is an enlargement of the gland, called *benign prostatic hyperplasia*, or BPH for short. The other is *prostatitis*, a bacterial infection. BPH is considerably more common, generally striking men after the age of 45. By the age 50, about 30 percent of all men will begin to experience difficulties stemming from an enlarged prostate. Problems associated with this disorder worsen with age, increasing in incidence to about 50 percent of all males by the age of sixty, and up to nearly 80 percent past the age of seventy.

The actual growth of the prostate tissue that results in BPH is caused by the hormone testosterone, which is produced by both the testicles and the adrenal glands. As a man ages, the conversion of testosterone to its more active form of dihydrotestosterone (DHT) becomes more prodigious. The consequences of DHT over-activity means an inordinate proliferation or growth of tissues in the prostate gland, which ultimately leads to the obstruction of the urethra, which passes through it.

Symptoms of BPH include an almost constant feeling for the need to urinate - particularly at night, reduced urination flow, the inability to completely empty the bladder, and even constipation. While this may not sound serious, the results of BPH can lead to an increased sense of frustration, embarrassment, and fatigue, as well as the complete disruption of normal activities.

The most common form of treatment of BPH by mainstream physicians are drugs, medical devices, and even surgery; in short, the symptoms rather than the disorder itself is addressed. While they may be a "quick fix," they can also come with some serious side effects.

If you believe you may have a prostate problem you must consult your doctor and ask that you be sent for a blood test to identify the prostatic specific antigen level (PSA test) of your prostate. Your doctor also performs what is known as a (DRE) digital rectum examination, where any enlargement of the prostate can be ascertained from this examination. The PSA test is a simple straight forward blood test. If the PSA level is above a level of 2.1 for men below 50 years and up to 4 for men above 50 years which is considered normal the doctor may consider several options

1. If the PSA level is low towards the norm, then watchful attention is considered and another PSA test would be ordered in 30 to 90 days, depending on the level.
2. You may be sent for a biopsy, which involves taking a tissue sample from the prostate gland, generally through the wall of the rectum. This tissue sample is then cultured in the laboratory and if there are any cancerous cells present an assessment is made of the growth pattern and an index given.

The PSA test is not considered a very accurate method of ascertaining if cancer is present, but for the moment it is the best the medical profession have. The number of false alarms with higher than average PSA levels is quite normal, very often due to a urinary tract infection that can be cleared up with an anti-biotic.

If however like me you have been diagnosed with prostate cancer then the following diet will help. The diet is designed to reduce the intake of immune system inhibitors (food preservatives etc). And, by supplying the body with omega-3 from flaxseed oil will benefit and optimise the immune response and may reduce secondary metastasis to vital organs especially the liver, lung and bone.

Omega-3 Protein Diet - An Aid For Prostate Problems
Avoid If Possible:
Anything that contains hydrogenated oil or fat, these include: Margarines, Spreads Commercial Vegetable Oils, and Salad Oils.
All processed Food that contain preservatives.
Non Foods such as refined sugars, sweetened jams, confectionary, orange juice in cartons (squeeze your own).
Pastries and Breads with refined flour or hydrogenated oils/fats from the bakers.
Pre-cooked meats, sausages and pates that contain preservatives.
Animal fats such as lard, dripping and suet.
Red meat and fresh meats should be organic or wild wherever possible. Dairy produce other than part of diet: Cheese, milk
In Moderation:
Chocolate: only Belgium milk chocolate
Butter
Tea, coffee and alcohol
Refer to 'Super Foods' section for some guide lines on what will give you that edge.

THE FIRST DAY ONLY
Start First Day In The Morning-Repeat At Midday and 6pm
- 5 tablespoons (80ml) of Flaxseed Oil mixed with 1 (15ml) tablespoon of honey and 1 glass of Purple Grape Juice **(Not For Diabetics)** or a glass of Champagne. Champagne has a positive benefit within this diet as it is easily absorbed. A little water to quench the thirst may be taken during this first day.
- 1 Tbsp Apple Cider Vinegar in water (compulsory)

No Sugar: Purple Grape Juice or honey must be taken for sweetening in place of sugar (Not Diabetics).
A Beverage 3 Times Per Day: 1 cup Peppermint, Rose Hip or Black or Green tea is allowed before midday. These may be sweetened to taste with honey.

THE DIET PLAN SHOULD CONTINUE EACH DAY AS FOLLOWS:

BEFORE BREAKFAST – These kick start the digestion with good intestinal bacteria. 150ml (1 glass) of the following:
- Buttermilk, Acidophilus Milk or Kombucha Tea
- 1 Tbsp Apple Cider Vinegar in water.

BREAKFAST – Breakfast should be light and wholesome. Fresh Fruit or Berries in Season, e.g. Blackberries, Cherries, Strawberries, Grated Apple. With a topping of Dessert Crème.
   Add 2 tablespoons of – Defatted Flax Flake or ground whole flaxseed to either a separate drink of choosing or to the Dessert Crème (p170) topping on the fruit. These are an important part of the diet.
   Beverage of Herbal Tea, Black Tea or Fresh Juice.

Or, **The Quick Fix Breakfast:** In a liquidiser add 100ml of water, one cored apple or pear, a handful of strawberries. Add two tablespoons of pre-ground flax seed or flaxseed flake and two tablespoons of flaxseed oil and 4 tablespoons of Yoghurt or Quark. Liquidise into a 'Smoothy' vary the fruit to your choice – Tastes great and is bursting with nutrition.

LUNCHEON
APPETISER
Small raw salad of choice - carrots, tomato, kohlrabi, grapes, celery or cauliflower. Horseradish, chives or parsley may be added for flavour. This may be as a salad on its own or combined as a wholemeal bread sandwich.
Before lunch take 1 tablespoon of Apple Cider Vinegar in a glass of water. This will aid digestion and is nutritionally beneficial.

LUNCH
Lunch can consist of home made chicken broth with vegetables and if available flaxseed bread. Add to broth, potatoes, barley, buckwheat, or millet. Superb nutritional value.
You may add flavour to the broth with mixed herbs.
Vary the type of vegetable, but always include some onion, tomato and carrot.
For a hearty meal, a baked jacket potato is always a favourite. By adding fresh chives, fresh parsley, caraway, or other herbs you will be increasing the nutritional value of your food. Only ever add parsley to a dish in the last 5 minutes of cooking.

DESSERT
Some fresh fruit or berries, try to vary from those used for breakfast. Add and cover fruit with Dessert Crème or eat crème separate. Vary the Dessert Crème with vanilla, refer to p170.

AFTERNOON (4PM) –
A small glass of organic red wine (no preservatives), purple grape juice or champagne with 1 heaped tablespoons of ground linseeds with honey to taste. Follow with (150ml) a glass of water.

EVENING MEAL/SUPPER –
This should be consumed no later than 7.30pm.
This may consist of:
Fish: Coldwater white fish such as cod, plaice, skate, halibut, sole or turbot. Avoid farmed reared salmon and trout.

Poultry: Chicken (without the skin), Rabbit, Turkey or wild game dish These should be grilled or baked. Refer to recipe and meal suggestions.

Beef or Lamb: Grilled or casseroled. (remove as much fat as possible). Include a jacket potato, pasta or rice with steamed green vegetables.

Quick supper:
An excellent nourishing supper is a homemade soup or broth with the chicken stock as the base. You may add Millet, Buckwheat or Oatmeal for extra nutrition.
Dessert:
A little fruit with a serving of Flax Dessert Crème, refer to p170

Fluid Intake: It is important to have no less than 2 litre of fluid per day. Taking into account fruit juices you will still need to have 8 glasses of water spread throughout the day. Avoid fluids 30 minutes either side of a meal as this will reduce the efficiency of digestive juices. Try not to take fluids after about 7pm if you normally visit the bathroom several times a night.

Purple Grape Juice: This has several beneficial effects, try to locate a good quality and drink two glasses per day. Purple grape juice has shown to increase Nitric Oxide (NO) by 70% in the body as well as having high anti-oxidant properties. Nitric Oxide dilates the blood vessels and has shown benefits with blood circulation to the extremities.

For The Healthy: You will need to consume no less than two to four tablespoons of flaxseed oil each day plus two tablespoons of ground whole flaxseed

Loose That Fat - Eat More Fat!

Before we start this next section, lets feed (excuse the pun) you some relevant information. It is almost physically impossible for the human body to loose more than one pound (450g) of fat in one week – absolutely impossible - even Shylock had a problem getting his pound of flesh. You may be able to loose more than six pounds in total weight during a week of dieting, but most of it will be water.

Let's start again – 'Loose that fat – Eat more fat!
That's correct - eat more fat, but lose more weight. Tell me more you ask! Well, you've tried just about every diet aficionado's book around. And now you have resigned yourself to the fact that your body is in a permanent state of self-destruct mode. Why else would your weigh have boomeranged back to the weight you were before you started the diet or even worse your weight has increased?
The reason is quite simple; your body is not in a state of self-destruct, but self-preservation and self-protection.
Why?
What happens is, when you begin to cut out calories to your body your genes identify this reduction as a possible famine situation and the body begins to make its own arrangements for survival, which you have no control over.
This is Mother Nature's way of allowing us to survive. This is a natural bodily instinct that is remembered by our genes going back to those pre-historic times, when our food rations were a little more scarce and not so easy to acquire as dropping into the corner store or popping round to the supermarket.
By dieting you are sub-consciously telling your body you are entering a period of famine and by reducing the amount of calorie intake you are also slowing down the metabolic rate of your body, because, your body is protecting itself by not burning off so many calories for energy. It is not infrequent for individuals on a diet to have reduced energy levels and feel somewhat lethargic due to the

body holding onto to those energy reserves. When you come out of a diet or an unintentional sub-conscious famine, the body starts to build up a storehouse of calories as body fat in expectation of the next diet (famine).

You'll see your weight begin to increase slowly and lo and behold your back to where you started – and another diet has gone out the window.

Get it – diets do not work.

Now for the bad news! The modern trend towards no or low fat foods has given us an under exercised population who are getting plumper and more obese. Recent research by nutritionists and the medical profession has identified more than one third of children of 5 years of age as officially being obese. Adults despite the increase in the number of gymnasiums and health fitness studios are getting bigger and bigger, or should I say plumper and plumper.

As we eat foods that are low fat or no fat we do not expect nor anticipate for these to increase our weight, but that's where we are wrong, because that is exactly what they do. Most of those invitingly, brightly packaged low fat or no-fat foods are refined, calorie dense, carbohydrates. Very often containing pretty nasty forms of hydrogenated oils or even worse trans fats and if you do not use these up in the production of energy with rigorous exercise, then they will be metabolised by the body into unwanted and unsightly fat tissue.

The Biochemists First Law – again!

Fat Burns In The Flame Of Carbohydrates

But you have to get it right. By balancing your fat, protein and carbohydrates intake and keeping them in harmony you will naturally burn fat with the metabolic processes of your body. Flaxseed oil and ground whole flaxseed increase that metabolic rate – enabling calories to be burnt off much easier rather than depositing them as stored fat. Omega-3 also has the ability to act as a solvent on saturated blood fats, keeping them mobile and reducing the amount deposited as adipose fats.

Fatty Facts
There is a vast amount of research and scientific data as to the health and nutritional benefits of flax seed oil and Omega-3, which has been covered briefly in this book.

There is however a caution with regards to using fish oil for supplementing your diet with Omega-3. Care must be taken with the ingestion of Omega-3 from fish oils (salmon, cod liver oil etc) – A recent study by *Greenpeace* reported with:
"Body of Evidence: The Effects Of Chlorine On Human Health":
'Relates that in independent laboratory analysis of 20 fish oil supplements, all of which had detectable amounts/levels of cancer causing organo-chlorine pesticides, including DDT and also the feared cancer causing polychlorinated biphenyls (PCB's)'.

So if you are supplementing with Omega-3 make sure it is a well sourced flax seed oil, preferably from Brown Canadian seed.

Getting back to the fat issue – Flax seed really is the 7th Calvary and is the hero in the battle against fat – by a fat.
A diet that is balanced nutritionally and high in fibre (whole flaxseed), rich in essential oils (flaxseed oil and borage oil) with nutritionally complete foods will give an individual optimal health and weight loss by removing unnecessary adipose fat tissue either by using the burning of calories by increasing the metabolic rate or by its solvent diluting type mechanism.

When Is A Fat Not A Fat?
When it's an essential fatty acid!
When we include flax seed oil and or flax seed flake as part of a meal, it tends to create a sensation of fullness (satiation). When flaxseed is ingested the components cause the stomach to retain foods for a longer period aiding digestion when compared to low

fat foods. With the inclusion of flaxseed oil to a diet it also results in a slower release of both food and flaxseed oil in combination into the small intestine. The body benefits from a gradual, slow rise in blood sugar, followed by the plateau effect and levelling of the blood sugars.

Finally the blood sugars undergo a controlled reduction within the blood. As a result of this improved metabolic rate there is a benefit of extended energy, stamina and satisfaction with no immediate hunger pangs following the meal.

The upshot is that you feel satisfied and will actually eat fewer calories in the long run than if you had chosen a low-fat diet... Simple really.

From personal experience I found that flax seed oil and flaxseed, substantially increased my metabolic rate, my energy increased and the blood profiles taken every 10 to 14 days improved one after another. By increasing my body's metabolic rate it was something like throwing more coals on the fire and once stoked, the system generated more heat, which in turn burnt off more calories as fuel, resulting in the reduction of unwanted body fats.

Omega-3 Protein Diet - An Aid To Weight Loss
Avoid If Possible:
Anything that contains hydrogenated oil/fat, these include: Margarines, spreads, commercial vegetable oils, salad oils.
Processed Food that contain preservatives.
Non Foods such as refined sugars, jams, confectionary, orange juice in cartons (squeeze own).
Pastries and breads with refined flour or hydrogenated oils/fats from the bakers.
Pre-cooked meats, sausages and pates that contain preservatives.
In Moderation:
Animal fats such as lard, dripping and suet (fresh only).
Red meat and fresh meats should be organic or wild wherever possible.
Chocolate: only Belgium milk chocolate.
Dairy: Butter, Cheese.
Refer to 'Super Foods' section for some guide lines on what will give you that edge.

THE FIRST DAY ONLY
Start First Day In The Morning- Repeat At Midday and 6pm
- 5 tablespoons (80ml) of Flaxseed Oil mixed with 1 (15ml) tablespoon of honey and 1 glass of Purple Grape Juice **(Not For Diabetics)** or a glass of Champagne.
  Champagne has a positive benefit within this diet as it is easily absorbed. A little water to quench the thirst may be taken during this first day.
- 1 Tbsp Apple Cider Vinegar in glass of water

No Sugar: Purple Grape Juice or honey must be taken for sweetening in place of sugar (Not Diabetics).
A Beverage 3 Times Per Day: 1 cup Peppermint, Rose Hip or Black or Green tea is allowed before midday. These may be sweetened to taste with honey.

THE DIET PLAN SHOULD CONTINUE EACH DAY AS FOLLOWS:

BEFORE BREAKFAST – These kick start the digestion with good intestinal bacteria. 150ml (1 glass) of the following:
- Buttermilk, Acidophilus Milk or Kombucha Tea

1 Tbsp Apple Cider Vinegar in glass of water (Compulsory)

BREAKFAST – Breakfast should be light and wholesome. Fresh Fruit or Berries in Season, e.g. Blackberries, Cherries, Grated Apple, Strawberries. With a topping of Dessert Crème (p170).
Add 2 tablespoons of – Defatted Flax Flake or ground whole flaxseed to either a separate drink of choosing or to the Dessert Crème (p170) topping on the fruit. These are an important part of the diet.
Beverage of Herbal Tea, Black Tea or Fresh Juice.

Or, **The Quick Fix Breakfast:** In a liquidiser add 100ml of water, one cored and peeled apple, one cored and peeled pear, a handful of strawberries. Add two tablespoons of pre-ground flax seed or flaxseed flake and two tablespoons of flaxseed oil and 4 tablespoons of Yoghurt or Quark. Liquidise into a 'Smoothey' vary the fruit to your choice – Taste's great and is bursting with nutrition.

MID MORNING TEA (10AM) –
150ml (wine glass) of pure fresh squeezed/juiced fruit juice

LUNCHEON
APPETISER
Small raw salad of choice - carrots, tomato, kohlrabi, grapes, celery or cauliflower. Horseradish, chives or parsley may be added for flavour. This may be as a salad on its own or combined as a wholemeal bread sandwich.
Before lunch take 1 tablespoon of Apple Cider Vinegar in a glass of water. This will aid digestion and is nutritionally beneficial

LUNCH
Lunch can consist of home made chicken broth with vegetables and if available flaxseed bread. Add to broth barley buckwheat or millet. Superb nutritional value.
You may add flavour to the broth with mixed herbs.
Vary the type of vegetable, but always include some onion, tomato and carrot.
For a hearty meal, a baked jacket potato is always a favourite. By adding fresh chives, fresh parsley, caraway, or other herbs you will be increasing the nutritional value of your food. Only ever add parsley to a dish in the last 5 minutes of cooking.

DESSERT – (compulsory)
Some fresh fruit or berries, try to vary from those used for breakfast. Add and cover fruit with Dessert Crème or eat crème separate. Vary the flavour of Dessert Crème with vanilla or cinnamon.

AFTERNOON (4PM) –
A small glass of organic red wine (no preservatives), purple grape juice or champagne with 1 heaped tablespoons of ground linseeds with honey to taste. Follow with (150ml) a glass of water.

EVENING MEAL/SUPPER –
This should be consumed no later than 8pm.
This may consist of:
Fish: Coldwater white fish such as cod, plaice, skate, halibut, sole or turbot – Grilled or Baked.
Avoid farmed reared salmon and trout.
Poultry: Chicken (without the skin), Rabbit, Turkey or wild game dish. These should be grilled or baked. *Refer to recipe and meal suggestions.*
Beef or Lamb: Grilled or casseroled. (remove as much fat as possible). Include a jacket potato, pasta or rice with steamed green vegetables.
Quick supper:

An excellent nourishing supper is a homemade soup or broth with the chicken stock as the base. You may add Millet, Buckwheat or Oatmeal for extra nutrition.

Dessert:
A little fruit with a serving of Flax Dessert Crème.

Fluid Intake: It is important to have no less than 2 litre of fluid per day. Taking into account fruit juices you will still need to have 8 glasses of water spread throughout the day. Avoid fluids 30 minutes either side of a meal as this will reduce the efficiency of digestive juices.

Purple Grape Juice: This has several beneficial effects, try to locate a good quality and drink two glasses per day. Purple grape juice has shown to increase Nitric Oxide (NO) by 70% in the body as well as having high anti-oxidant properties. Nitric Oxide dilates the blood vessels and has shown benefits with blood circulation to the extremities.

Weight Loss/Optimisation: Through the course of each day you are looking to consume no less than four tablespoons of flaxseed oil with a protein such as quark or yoghurt plus at least 3 tablespoons of ground whole flaxseed or flaxseed flake.

For The Healthy: You will need to consume no less than two to four tablespoons of flaxseed oil each day plus two tablespoons of ground whole flaxseed

Arthritis – Flax Seed A Potential Aid

The pain associated with arthritis is caused by the inflammation of tissue surrounding the joints that includes tendons, ligaments, and cartilage. There are several forms of arthritic conditions all of which are extremely uncomfortable and most often painful.

They are:
Rheumatoid Arthritis
With this debilitating condition, joints, knees and most commonly the small joints of the hand become very tender, swollen and eventually possibly deformed. The disease is thought to be caused by own auto-immune system condition, wherein our own immune response attacks our joints.

Osteoarthritis
is a gradual degeneration of the large primary weight bearing bones and joints.

Gout
is most frequently due to diet irregularities that are high in animal fats and meats. The actual cause is when the level of uric acid rises to unhealthy levels in the body, it then crystallises causing needle-like pain.

Arthritis has been around for centuries afflicting a major proportion of elderly individuals and as a result of our modern day diet it is afflicting younger people. Arthritis is known to affect almost every part of the body: from the fingers to the shoulders – from the back to the knee and the hips down to the feet. Pain that is associated with arthritis can be from a slight nagging dull pain and stiffness of the joints with some swelling to a chronic crippling disability.
Many people who are suffering with arthritis have varying levels and may not necessarily be restricted to one type of of the disease. Never the less, regardless of the type of arthritis, the end result is pain and inflammation.

This continual debilitating pain, which sufferers have to endure has led to the explosion of pharmaceutical led drugs, prescribed medications to control the joint inflammation, which when effective will reduce inflammation and the associated pain.

Many of the prescribed drugs work by interfering with our hormone-like compounds – prostaglandins, as I mentioned earlier some extremely important work in the body is fulfilled by prostaglandins, what we do not want to do is interfere with their beneficial work on the body..

Some of the anti-inflammatory medications prescribed for arthritic conditions come with long-term side effects, as I can attest to, as I had to use something similar for reducing inflammation with my illness, they are not very nice.

By continually using pharmaceutical medications, they may even lead to a worsening of the arthritic condition, as you are treating the symptoms – not the illness.

A Powerful Anti-Inflammatory Agent – Omega 3

For a healthy individual the anti-inflammatory prostaglandins are produced from their dietary ingestion of Omega-3 from seed oils such as flax seed, or deep-water fish.

This immune system inflammatory response within our body is regulated by these prostaglandins.

Omega-3 oils sometimes referred to as a Essential Fatty Acids, sometimes as a super-polyunsaturated oil – what ever you want to call them, the scientists have proven that it is one of natures most powerful anti-inflammatory agents.

A diet which is high in Omega-6 rich oils, such as corn, safflower, and sunflower, as well as animal fats and meats, can lead to the production of prostaglandins that are inflammatory by nature, which will result in a serious worsening of the inflammatory conditions. With the high occurrence of arthritic illness and many other inflammatory related conditions, it is possible that these illnesses and ailments may be due to a diet that is excessively high in Omega-6 laden oils and animal meats in proportion to the amount of Omega-3 fatty acids we consume.

This shift in our dietary habits towards the prominence of omega-6 over omega-3 has been well documented over the past 100 years. One study concluded that arthritics suffer from a 50% deficiency in essential fatty acids compared to other non-effected individuals. The problem is that our modern western diet has caused a deficiency in 90% of the population in Britain.

There is a big difference in the pharmaceutical approach to alleviating painful inflammatory conditions associated with arthritis and those by ingesting with Omega-3.

Importantly, Omega 3 has none of the side effects that come with the use of pharmaceutical medications. The concern of many arthritic sufferers even those in the early stages is the possibility of the disease developing to a chronic stage of severe rheumatoid arthritic condition.

Is that the 7th Cavalry I see on the horizon.

Help is at hand with flaxseed oil and it's companion Omega-3 and that is not all, there are no side effects.

Having the power to regulate prostaglandins, Omega-3 oils benefits the body by aiding the optimisation of the immune system, reducing the severity of autoimmune response conditions, which includes rheumatoid arthritis.

The Overview:
- Essential fatty acids modulate the immune system, thereby suppressing the attack by our own immune cells on bones, cartilage and tissues of the body.
- Essential fatty acids (Omega-3) decrease the inflammatory response through the production of hormone-like compounds called prostaglandins.

The evidence suggests that it would be most beneficial for arthritic suffers to supplement with essential fatty acids such as Omega-3.

The benefits they would find:
- **Reduction in the progression of the illness and degeneration of joints through optimisation and modulation of the immune system.**
- **Reduction of pain associated with arthritis by lessening inflammation to the affected area.**
- **Enhance the quality of life.**

Omega-3 Protein Diet - An Aid For Arthritis

Avoid:
Anything that contains hydrogenated oil or fat, these include: Margarines, Spreads Commercial Vegetable Oils, Salad Oils.
Processed Food that contain preservatives.
Non Foods such as refined sugars, jams, confectionary, orange juice in cartons (squeeze own).
Pastries and breads with refined flour or hydrogenated oils/fats from the bakers.
Pre-cooked meats, sausages and pates that contain preservatives.
Animal fats such as lard, dripping and suet (fresh only).
Red meat and fresh meats should be organic or wild wherever possible.
Chocolate: only Belgium milk chocolate, low in sugar.
Dairy: Butter, Cheese.
Alcohol.
Fresh fruit in moderation.

Refer to 'Super Foods' section for some guide lines on what will give you that edge.

Arthritis and Alkaline Reducing Diet

This is an excellent diet if you suffer with over acidity of the body. This diet is also recommended for sufferers of osteo-arthritis and rheumatoid arthritis where it is thought that toxic acids have accumulate at the joints, thus causing painful inflammation. It is believed that these acids originate from the intestines when in excess quantities. The body's normal metabolic process has failed to detoxify them so they end up in the joint.
It is also useful to include a digestive enzyme with this diet as that may also aid in reducing the effects of arthritis and acidity.

	Foods to avoid		Foods allowed
1	Red meat	1	White fish, trout, salmon (no bottom feeding fish), Beans, peas, pulses, and lentils. Chicken - 2 meals per week Eggs - 2 meals of 2 eggs per week
2	Cow's milk, cheese & yoghurt	2	Goat's milk, Quark, Cheese & Yoghurt
3	White or brown wheat flour Wheat bran or any product containing these. Or, any produce that may contain edible starch, cereal filler and cereal protein.	3	Oats, brown rice, corn, maize, buckwheat pasta, millet, pure rye crisp bread, sugar free muesli, sugar free oat cakes
4	Waxed covered Citrus fruit, such as lemon, apple etc	4	All organic fruit. Dried fruit. Tomatoes twice a week only
5		5	All vegetables The darker the green the better. Above ground crop more than root
6	Dry roasted nuts. Peanuts	6	Almonds, Cashew, Walnut,. Hazel and, Pine nuts
7	Refined sugar, syrup, treacle and honey.	7	Dried fruit, Cane Molasses, and Sugar free jams
8	Alcohol, Tea, Cocoa, Coffee.	8	Herbal teas, Unsweetened fruit juice (pure), Vegetable juices.
9	Margarine Butter use sparingly.	9	Only Unrefined Pure Extra Virgin Olive Oil,

Do Not:

Eat <u>ANY</u> fried or deep fried food. This increases the acid level in the body.

Eat any fast foods or junk foods. Increases acidity as well as being lower in nutrition.

Reheat food from the previous day. This reduces the amount of oxygen available from the food thus increasing the acidity of the body.

THE FIRST DAY ONLY
Start First Day In The Morning- Repeat At Midday and 6pm
- 5 tablespoons (80ml) of Flaxseed Oil mixed low sugar fruit juice or a glass of Champagne. Champagne has a positive benefit within this diet as it is easily absorbed. A little water to quench the thirst may be taken during this first day.
- 1 Tbsp of Apple Cider Vinegar in glass of water

No Sugar...
A Beverage 3 Times Per Day: 1 cup Peppermint, Rose Hip or Black or Green tea is allowed before midday.

THE DIET PLAN SHOULD CONTINUE EACH DAY AS FOLLOWS:

BEFORE BREAKFAST – These kick start the digestion with good intestinal bacteria. 150ml (1 glass) of the following:
- Buttermilk, Acidophilus Milk or Kombucha Tea

1 Tbsp Apple Cider Vinegar in glass of water (Compulsory)

BREAKFAST – Breakfast should be light and wholesome. Fresh Fruit or Berries in Season, e.g. Blackberries, Cherries, Strawberries, Grated Apple or Pear.
With a topping of Flax/Dessert Crème.
> Add 3 tablespoons of – Defatted Flax Flake or ground whole flaxseed to either a separate drink of choosing or to the Dessert Crème topping on the fruit. These are an important part of the diet.
> Beverage of Herbal Tea, Black Tea or Fresh Juice.

Or, **The Quick Fix Breakfast:** In a liquidiser add 100ml of water, one peeled and cored pear a handful of strawberries or berries. Add three tablespoons of pre-ground flax seed or flaxseed flake and two tablespoons of flaxseed oil and 4 tablespoons of Yoghurt or Quark. Liquidise into a 'Smoothy' vary the fruit to your choice – Tastes great and is bursting with nutrition.

MID MORNING TEA (10AM) –
150ml (wine glass) of Kombucha Tea or a glass of pure fresh squeezed/juiced fruit juice

LUNCHEON
APPETISER
Small raw salad of choice - carrots, tomato, kohlrabi, grapes, celery or cauliflower. Horseradish, chives or parsley may be added for flavour. This may be as a salad on its own or combined as a wholemeal bread sandwich.

Before lunch take 1 tablespoon of Apple Cider Vinegar in a glass of water. This will aid digestion and is nutritionally beneficial

LUNCH – COOKED (optional)
Lunch can consist of home made chicken broth with vegetables and if available flaxseed bread. Add to broth, potatoes, barley, buckwheat or millet. Superb nutritional value.

You may add flavour to the broth with soy sauce or mixed herbs.

Vary the type of vegetable, but always include some onion and carrot.

For a hearty meal, a baked jacket potato is always a favourite. By adding fresh chives, fresh parsley, caraway, or other herbs you will be increasing the nutritional value of your food. Only ever add parsley to a dish in the last 5 minutes of cooking.

DESSERT – (compulsory)
Some fresh berries, try to vary from those used for breakfast. Add and cover fruit with Dessert Crème or eat crème separate. Vary the Dessert Crème with vanilla, refer to p170.

AFTERNOON (4PM) –
A small glass of organic red wine (no preservatives) or champagne with 1 heaped tablespoons of ground linseeds. Follow with (150ml) a glass of water.

AFTERNOON – 1 HOUR BEFORE SUPPER (5PM-6PM)
1 glass (150ml) of Kombucha Tea (optional) or Fresh squeezed fruit juice.

EVENING MEAL/SUPPER –

This should be consumed no later than 7pm.

This may consist of:
Fish: Coldwater white fish such as cod, plaice, skate, halibut, sole or turbot. Avoid farmed reared salmon and trout.

Poultry: Chicken (without the skin), Rabbit, Turkey or wild game dish These should be grilled or baked. *Refer to recipe section.*

Quick supper:
An excellent nourishing supper is a homemade soup or broth with the chicken stock as the base. You may add Millet, Buckwheat or Oatmeal for extra nutrition.
Dessert:
Some fresh berries with a serving of Flax Dessert Crème p170.

AFTER 30 DAYS you may add dishes of Beef or Lamb: Grilled or casseroled. (remove as much fat as possible). If the arthritic condition begins to return then you must remove red meat totally from your diet.

Fluid Intake: It is important to have no less than 2 litre of fluid per day. Taking into account juices you will still need to have 8 glasses of water spread throughout the day. Avoid fluids 30 minutes either side of a meal as this will reduce the efficiency of digestive juices.

Lowering Cholesterol And Blood Pressure

Heart attacks, strokes, and associated cardiovascular diseases that relate to atherosclerosis are responsible for about 40% of all mortalities in Western Society. Atherosclerosis is not something that happens over-night, it is a condition that is degenerative which has built up over a period of many years. Atherosclerosis of the arteries can simply be described as an accumulation of lipids (fats) in the arteries that are sticking to the artery wall.
When these fats begin to adhere to the artery walls with what is known as atherosclerotic plaque, or atheroma, the most likely outcome unless treated will be cardiovascular disease leading to premature death. Almost any artery in the body may be affected, but it is normally the aorta, coronary and arteries supplying the brain that are most often involved.
Most individuals who suffer with cardiovascular diseases are as a result of atherosclerosis or hardening of the artery walls. Cardiovascular (heart) disease is most often referred to as a restriction or blockage of the coronary arteries, and those that supply the heart with oxygen and primary nutrients. A heart attack is actually a restriction in arterial the blood flow via the arteries connecting to the heart. If these arteries become severely blocked due to a build up of the cholesterol laden plaque, severe damage to the heart may result or even death of the heart muscle.

**Atherosclerosis and associated complications
are a preventable condition with the correct diet.**

Atherosclerosis And Cholesterol
The overwhelmingly scientific medical evidence demonstrates that elevated cholesterol levels, which are left undiagnosed or untreated are extremely dangerous if not deadly.
Firstly, we must understand that our body's need cholesterol as it plays such an important and vital role in certain metabolic functions which include the production of bile acids and sex hormones.

Cholesterol is transported in the blood by molecules known as lipoproteins. The first course of action in preventing and the treatment of heart disease and strokes is to lower the blood cholesterol levels.

However, not all cholesterol is bad; Cholesterol bound to low density lipoprotein (LDL) is often referred to as the villain or bad cholesterol while cholesterol bound to high density lipoprotein (HDL) is the guy nominated as good cholesterol.

LDL cholesterol in our bodies increases the risk of heart disease, strokes, and high blood pressure whilst HDL cholesterol has beneficial effects on the body by protecting us against heart disease.

LDL transports and dumps cholesterol to the tissues. HDL, on the other hand, transports cholesterol to the liver for metabolism and excretion from the body. Therefore our LDL-to-HDL ratio signifies if cholesterol is being dumped into our tissues or broken down by the liver and then excreted. So the most important aid which we can give our bodies is to reduce the level of LDL cholesterol whilst at the same time raising our HDL cholesterol levels.

Omega-3 Oils and Cholesterol

There are numerous scientific studies that have shown the normalization of blood lipids (fats) in hyper-lipidemic individuals when supplementing with Omega-3 fatty acids. Omega-3 fatty acids have the ability to break down cholesterol in the lining of blood vessels, as well as keeping saturated fats from our diet mobile in the blood. The end result is less cholesterol in the body and blood stream, and a reduced likelihood of cholesterol/heart disease related complications in the future.

Omega-3 Oils and Blood Pressure

Your heart pumps blood into your circulation every time it beats, that creates a pulse you can feel in the arteries near to the skin surface of your neck, arm or wrist. During the peak (the beat) reading of the pressure exerted by this contraction is the systolic

pressure. Between beats the heart will relax and accordingly blood pressure drops.
The very lowest reading is known as the diastolic pressure. A normal blood pressure reading for an adult is about 120 (systolic) / 80 (diastolic).

Pulse Guide

	Low BP	Normal BP	Watchful BP	High BP
Systolic		110	140	160
Diastolic		50-60	90	95

Very high blood pressure is dangerous for health increasing the risk of the major risk factors for a heart attack or stroke. Since heart disease and strokes combined account for over 40% of all deaths in the U.K., it is very important to keep the blood pressure in the normal range. The watchful level in the table above of 140/80 is indicative of high blood pressure or hypertension.

Dietary factors appear to be the primary cause of blood pressure related illness. What is referred to as resting blood pressure generally rises with age and does not happen over night, it takes many years before it rises above a critical level whereupon it tends to damage blood vessels, thickening them and increasing their resistance. Under these conditions it forces the heart to beat harder, thus increasing blood pressure which further creates a vicious spiral to potential disaster.

If you are able to detect a small increase in the rise in blood pressure early then you are likely to prevent the onset of a potentially life threatening disease.

Other than attaining an ideal body weight and exercising on a regular basis, perhaps the most important dietary recommendation is to increase the consumption of vegetable, fruit and plant foods in the diet. Vegetarians have a lower incidence of cardiovascular disease and typically a vegetarians diet has more essential fatty acids, complex carbohydrates, fibre, calcium, magnesium, vitamin

C and no animal and lower saturated fat in their diet. This type of diet has a much more favourable influence on reducing blood pressure.

There is no need to go to a vegetarian diet, there is the simple supplementing of your diet with flax seed oil which will increase the ratio of Omega-3 fatty acids which will enable you to lower your blood pressure by making the blood more slippery.

There many cardiovascular, blood pressure and cholesterol studies that have findings showing that fish oil, cod liver oil or flax seed oil all presenting Omega-3 to the body are very effective in lower blood pressure.

Flax seed oil is the better choice for lowering blood pressure, especially when cost effectiveness is a consideration.

Also it has been shown that some commercially available fish oils and cod liver oils can contain very high levels of lipid peroxides (rancid oil) which greatly stresses the antioxidant defence mechanisms, at this time it makes the most sense to rely on cold water fish and flaxseed oil for the Omega-3 oils rather than fish oil capsules. Cold water fish however although a good source, to get to the level high enough for therapeutic results, you'll need a good appetite as the concentrations of Omega-3 in fresh cold water fish is at least five fold lower than that in flaxseed oil.

Summary

The beneficial effects of Omega-3 oils in protecting as well as treating cardiovascular disease are quite obvious. Omega-3 oils have many factors linked to heart attacks and strokes. They lower both systolic and diastolic blood pressure in individuals with high blood pressure, they lower LDL-cholesterol levels and triglycerides as well as fibrinogen levels and inhibit excessive platelet aggregation (clumping and sticking).

Omega-3 Protein Diet - An Aid To Reducing Blood Pressure

Avoid:
Anything that contains hydrogenated oil or fat, these include: Margarines, Spreads Commercial Vegetable Oils, Salad Oils.
Processed Food that contain preservatives.
Non Foods such as refined sugars, sweetened jams, confectionary, orange juice in cartons (squeeze your own).
Pastries and Breads with refined flour or hydrogenated oils/fats from the bakers.
Pre-cooked meats, sausages and pates that contain preservatives.

In Moderation:
Animal fats such as lard, dripping and suet (fresh only).
Red meat and fresh meats should be organic or wild wherever possible.
Chocolate: only Belgium milk chocolate.
Dairy: Butter, Cheese.   *Refer to 'Super Foods' section for some guide lines on what will give you that edge.*

THE FIRST DAY ONLY

Start First Day In The Morning- Repeat At Midday and 6pm
- 5 tablespoons (80ml) of Flaxseed Oil mixed with 1 (15ml) tablespoon of honey and 1 glass of Purple Grape Juice **(Not For Diabetics)** or a glass of Champagne. Champagne has a positive benefit within this diet as it is easily absorbed. A little water to quench the thirst may be taken during this first day.

No Sugar: Purple Grape Juice or honey must be taken for sweetening in place of sugar (Not Diabetics).

A Beverage 3 Times Per Day: 1 cup Peppermint, Rose Hip or Black or Green tea is allowed before midday. These may be sweetened to taste with honey.

THE DIET PLAN SHOULD CONTINUE EACH DAY AS FOLLOWS:

BEFORE BREAKFAST – These kick start the digestion with good intestinal bacteria. 150ml (1 glass) of either of the following: Buttermilk, Acidophilus Milk or Kombucha Tea

BREAKFAST – Breakfast should be light and wholesome. Fresh Fruit or Berries in Season, e.g. Blackberries, Cherries, Grated Apple, Strawberries. With a topping of Dessert Crème - see p170.

> Add 2 tablespoons of – Defatted Flax Flake or ground whole flaxseed to either a separate drink of choosing or to the Dessert Crème topping on the fruit. These are an important part of the diet. Beverage of Herbal Tea, Black Tea or Fresh Juice.

Or, **The Quick Fix Breakfast:** In a liquidiser add 100ml of water, one peled and cored apple or pear, a handful of strawberries. Add two tablespoons of pre-ground flax seed or flaxseed flake and two tablespoons of flaxseed oil and 4 tablespoons or Yoghurt or Quark. Liquidise into a 'Smoothy' vary the fruit to your choice – Tastes great and is bursting with nutrition.

MID MORNING TEA (10AM) –

150ml (wine glass) of Kombucha Tea or a glass of pure fresh squeezed/juiced fruit juice

LUNCHEON

APPETISER

Small raw salad of choice - carrots, tomato, kohlrabi, grapes, celery or cauliflower. Horseradish, chives or parsley may be added for flavour. This may be as a salad on its own or combined as a wholemeal bread sandwich.

Before lunch take 1 tablespoon of Apple Cider Vinegar in a glass of water. This will aid digestion and is nutritionally beneficial

LUNCH – COOKED (optional)

Lunch can consist of home made chicken broth with vegetables and if available flaxseed bread. Add to broth, potatoes, buckwheat, barley or millet. Superb nutritional value.

You may add flavour to the broth with mixed herbs.
Vary the type of vegetable, but always include some onion, tomato and carrot.
For a hearty meal, a baked jacket potato is always a favourite. By adding fresh chives, fresh parsley, caraway, or other herbs you will be increasing the nutritional value of your food. Only ever add parsley to a dish in the last 5 minutes of cooking.

DESSERT – (compulsory)
Some fresh fruit or berries, try to vary from those used for breakfast. Add and cover fruit with Dessert Crème or eat crème separate. Vary the Dessert Crème with vanilla refer to p170.
AFTERNOON (4PM) – A small glass of organic red wine (no preservatives), purple grape juice or champagne with 1 heaped tablespoons of ground linseeds with honey to taste. Follow with (150ml) a glass of water.
AFTERNOON – 1 HOUR BEFORE SUPPER (5PM-6PM)
1 Tbsp of Apple Cider Vinegar in a glass of water

EVENING MEAL/SUPPER –
This should be consumed no later than 7.00pm.
This may consist of:
Fish: Coldwater white fish such as cod, plaice, skate, halibut, sole or turbot. Avoid farmed reared salmon and trout.
Poultry: Chicken (without the skin), Rabbit, Turkey or wild game dish These should be grilled or baked. Refer to recipe and meal suggestions.
Beef or Lamb: (No more than 100g twice per week) Grilled or casseroled. (remove all fat). Include a jacket potato, pasta or rice with steamed green vegetables.
Quick supper:
An excellent nourishing supper is a homemade soup or broth with the chicken stock as the base. You may add Millet, Buckwheat or Oatmeal for extra nutrition.

Dessert:
A little fruit with a serving of Flax Dessert Crème.

Fluid Intake: It is important to have no less than 2 litre of fluid per day. Taking into account fruit juices you will still need to have 8 glasses of water spread throughout the day. Avoid fluids 30 minutes either side of a meal as this will reduce the efficiency of digestive juices.

Purple Grape Juice: This has several beneficial effects, try to locate a good quality and drink two glasses per day. Purple grape juice has shown to increase Nitric Oxide (NO) by 70% in the body as well as having high anti-oxidant properties. Nitric Oxide dilates the blood vessels and has shown benefits with blood circulation to the extremities.

Preventing Heart Attacks & Strokes

Heart disease has risen over the past 60 years to become the leading killer in western society, taking an estimated 750,000 lives per year in the USA alone. This largely preventable malady continues to take its toll on lives here and abroad as people of other industrialised countries adopt similar eating habits of their American counterparts. Yet, in the 1920's the incidence of heart disease in the U.S.A. was so low that when a Mr P.D. White offered the medical profession an electrocardiogram device from Europe, he was dismissed by the medical profession, who believed the machine had little if any value for the medical profession.
But, in less than one generation of only 20 years or so the increase in heart disease in the North America was so dramatic that the device was acclaimed as a most desirable diagnostic tool.
Many scientific researchers now believe that the change in diet between 1915 (the introduction of margarine) and the 1940's was responsible for the substantial increase in heart related diseases. One of those changes that affected most peoples diet was a swing towards margarines and processed hydrogenated oils and fats in place of the much-maligned natural saturated fats such as butter.

Why Are Trans Fats And Hydrogenated Oils Bad?
Saturated and trans fats (hydrogenated oils such as those found in margarine) possess an ability to stack up and clump together (conglomerate) platelets in the blood, thus thickening the blood and making it more sticky. The action of thickening the blood creates a rise in blood pressure, which results in an increase in the workload and work rate of the heart. The problems associated with work rate of the heart begins to complicate the cardiovascular problem. The sticking and stacking ability of TFAs (Trans Fatty Acids) and also those of hydrogenated oils elevates and increases the build up of atherosclerotic plaque on the artery walls that lead to and from the heart muscle. When this begins to occur, the availability of life sustaining oxygen to the heart is

likely to be reduced, causing angina pectoris (blockage) and, possibly a heart attack.
Scientific research findings indicate very clearly that refined oils and processed fats such as trans fatty acids (TFA) found in many processed foods, have been shown to significantly elevate the harmful cholesterol low density lipoproteins (LDL), while at the same time decreasing the beneficial cholesterol high density lipoprotein (HDL) and increasing triglycerides.

In contrast to some dietary fat sources such as saturated and pseudo (hydrogenated oils) fats, Omega-3 family of fatty acids have been scientifically proven to reduce blood platelet stickiness (aggregation), and at the same time allowing saturated fats to become mobile in the blood stream, thus reducing the tendency for them to conglomerate or stick to the arterial muscle walls. The ability of omega-3 to benefit blood viscosity, allows a decrease in the workload on the heart. Therefore, a regular dietary intake of omega-3 will assist and aid in the balancing of metabolism and the production of prostaglandin, resulting in the regulation of proper arterial constriction and relaxation.

Omega-3 and Omega-6 are the fatty acids that are identified as the precursors for the hormone-like substances such as prostaglandins. These hormone-like substances are subject of many vitally important functions within the body and one of them is the regulating effect on our heart's artery muscle tone. If there is any disturbance created by a deficiency essential fatty acids this may well disrupt our body's systemic balance, which will give rise to arterial muscle spasm.
The modern western diet is unnecessarily heavily overloaded with omega-6 so all we need is a sensible supplementation of omega-3. In Britain it is estimated that this overload is in a ratio of possibly 8:1 whereas it should be in the region of about 5:1.

The Spiralling Effect Downwards:

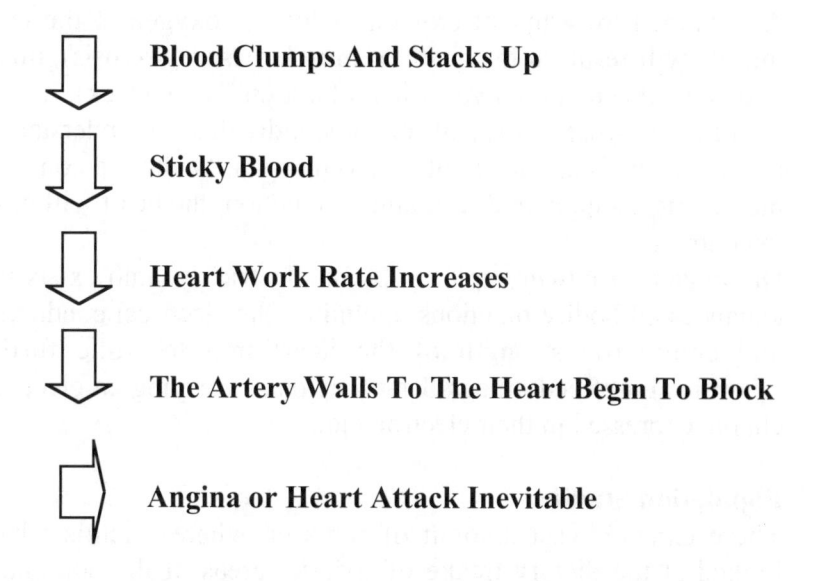

⬇ **Blood Clumps And Stacks Up**

⬇ **Sticky Blood**

⬇ **Heart Work Rate Increases**

⬇ **The Artery Walls To The Heart Begin To Block**

➡ **Angina or Heart Attack Inevitable**

The resulting increased work on the heart muscle can lead to an enlargement of the right ventricle (cor pulmonale). Now you may understand why this spiralling effect is so problematical for our health and is it any wonder why heart disease kills more people than all the other degenerative diseases combined?

How Does Omega 3 Work On The Heart
Scientific research and studies have recognised in their findings that there is a normalisation of blood lipids (fats) with hyperlipidemic (too much fat) people when they have been given Omega-3 fatty acids. The Omega 3 is known to decrease the harmful LDL cholesterol, and at the same time elevates the more favourable HDL (good) cholesterol, and also reduces the levels of triglyceride.

Omega-3 can be best described as the transporter or the shipping company for ferrying oxygen from haemoglobin (the oxygen carriers in red blood cells) to each and every one of our one hundred trillion cells.

A sustained lowering of oxygen or loss of oxygen to the heart muscle will result in the death of muscle tissue (necrosis), this is known medically as a myocardial infarction (heart attack).

And finally, what is difficult for some individuals to understand is that the heart is an electrically driven organ. Without a continual bioelectrical supply and resultant conduction, the heart will cease to contract.

Dr. Johanna Budwig explains "A bioelectric dynamo exists that enhances all bodily functions, including the electrical conduction and contractile strength of the heart muscle". She further identifies unrefined omega-3 fatty acids as carrying an electrical charge expressed in their electron cloud.

Population Studies

There exists a vast amount of research where scientists have looked at the dietary intake of specific areas of the population from different parts of the globe to explain why some types develop heart disease and others have a much lower incidence. These studies have demonstrated that people who consume a diet rich in Omega-3 oils from either cod water fish or vegetable sources have a significantly reduced risk of developing heart disease. Researchers also looked at the findings from autopsy studies. These revealed that the highest level of coronary artery disease is found in people with the lowest concentration of Omega-3 oils in their fat tissues. On the other hand, individuals with tissue saturation of omega-3 concentration, had the lowest degree of coronary artery disease.

We must therefore bare in mind that it may be assumed from these indicative findings that there is a likelyhood that by consuming adequate amounts of omega 3 oils as part of a regular diet may prevent heart attacks.

How about those individuals who already have heart disease?
Are those individuals who have experienced a heart attack and survived it, are they likely to experience another?
The Answer Is Yes!
That being the case is it possible for a regular diet rich in Omega-3 oils to prevent future heart related problem and heart attacks.
The Answer Is Yes!
There are numerous studies that have sought to determine if dietary alteration can prevent recurrence. In particular three of those studies back in the mid 90's have shown that dietary modifications involving Omega 3 are positively effective.

Is Vegetarianism The Answer?
Not entirely. One of the studies investigated the effects on the heart of a strict vegetarian diet. The findings indicated that a vegetarian diet is not as important as consuming a diet high in fibre and complex carbohydrates, and a little lower in saturated fat and cholesterol; although it is well known that vegetarians have a lower risk of developing heart disease. A vegetarian diet has been shown to be efficient in reducing the risk for atherosclerosis, lowering cholesterol levels and blood pressure. Such a diet is rich in a number of protective factors such as fibre, essential fatty acids (including higher levels of Omega-3 fatty acids), vitamins, and minerals including potassium and magnesium.
As for the other two studies the Dietary And Re-infarction Trial (DART) determined that increasing (supplementing) with Omega 3 fatty acids reduced the occurrence of future heart attacks.
And finally the Lyon Diet Heart Study often referred to as the Cretan Diet indicated that increasing the intake of Omega-3 from vegetable sources such as that found in flaxseed oil, offered the same level of protection as increasing cold water fish intake. These studies did fly in the face of dietary recommendation of the American Heart Association.

Summary

The beneficial effects of Omega-3 oils in protecting as well as treating cardiovascular disease are quite obvious. Omega-3 oils impacted on many numerous issues linked to heart attacks and strokes. They lower LDL-cholesterol levels and triglycerides; inhibit excessive platelet aggregation; lower both systolic and diastolic blood pressure in individuals with high blood pressure.

Flaxseed Oil and Flaxseed Flake has twice the available Omega 3 than Cod Liver Oil and it offers the most cost effective and beneficial method for increasing the intake of Omega-3 oils in the diet, and is a 100% natural vegetable source with none of the contamination problems associated with fish oils.

Stroke – A Preventable Malady

A stroke or "brain attack" occurs when a blood clot blocks a blood vessel or artery, or when a blood vessel breaks, interrupting blood flow to an area of the brain starving the area of oxygen (ischemia literally means 'keeping back blood'). When a stroke occurs, it kills brain cells in the immediate area.

This area of dead cells is known as an infarct. The cells within the effected area usually die within minutes to a few hours after the onset of a stroke.

When brain cells in the infarction die, they release chemicals that set off a chain reaction called the "ischemic cascade" This chain reaction endangers brain cells in a larger, surrounding area of brain tissue for which the blood supply is compromised but not completely cut off. Without prompt medical treatment this larger area of brain cells, called the penumbra, will also die. Given the rapid pace of the ischemic cascade, the "window of opportunity" for interventional treatment is about six hours.

Beyond this window, reestablishment of blood flow and administration of neuro protective agents may fail to help and can potentially cause further damage.

When brain cells die, control of abilities, which that area of the brain once controlled are lost. This includes functions such as speech, movement, and memory. The specific abilities lost or affected depend on where in the brain the stroke occurs and on the size of the stroke (i.e., the extent of brain cell death). For example, someone who has a small stroke may experience only minor effects such as weakness of an arm or leg. On the other hand, someone who has a larger stroke may be left paralysed on one side or lose his/her ability to express and process language. Some people recover completely from less serious strokes, while other individuals lose their lives to very severe strokes.

Changing the Perception of Stroke

Untrue: Stroke is unpreventable
Stroke only strikes the aging
Stroke has no treatment programme
Stroke is caused by the heart
Stroke recovery only happens for a few months

True: Stroke is a "Brain Attack"
Stroke is often preventable
Stroke needs emergency treatment
Stroke can happen to anyone
Stroke recovery continues throughout life

Atrial Fibrillation and other Heart Diseases

Heart disease such as atrial fibrillation increases stroke risk up to six times. About 15 percent of all people who have a stroke have a heart disease called atrial fibrillation, or AF, which affects more than 1 million Americans. AF is caused when the atria (the two upper chambers of the heart) beat rapidly and unpredictably, producing an irregular heartbeat. AF raises stroke risk because it allows blood to pool in the heart. When blood pools, it tends to form clots, which can then be carried to the brain, causing a stroke.

Normally, all four chambers of the heart beat in the same rhythm somewhere between 60 and 100 times every minute. In someone who has AF, the left atrium may beat as many as 400 times a minute. If left untreated, AF can increase stroke risk four to six times. Long-term untreated AF can also weaken the heart, leading to potential heart failure. The prevalence of AF increases with age. AF is found most often in people over age 65 and in people who have heart disease or thyroid disorders.

Coronary Heart Disease and High Cholesterol
High cholesterol can directly and indirectly increase stroke risk by clogging blood vessels and putting individuals at greater risk of coronary heart disease, another important stroke risk factor.

Sleep Disordered Breathing - Sleep Apnea
Sleep apnea is a major cardiovascular and stroke risk factor increasing blood pressure rates which may cause stroke or heart attack. Studies also indicate that people with sleep apnea develop dangerously low levels of oxygen in the blood while carbon dioxide levels rise, possibly causing blood clots or even strokes to occur. Diagnosing sleep apnea early may be an important stroke prevention tool.

Increase Stroke Risk Include:
High Blood Pressure
Having high blood pressure, or hypertension, increases stroke risk four to six times. It is the single most important controllable stroke risk factor. High blood pressure is often called "the silent killer" because people can have it and not realise it, since it often has no symptoms. Blood pressure is high if it is consistently more than 140/90. Between 50 and 90 percent of all stroke patients had high blood pressure before their stroke. Hypertension puts stress on blood vessel walls and can lead to strokes from blood clots or haemorrhage.

Smoking: Smoking doubles stroke risk. Smoking damages blood vessel walls, speeds up the clogging of arteries by deposits, raises blood pressure and makes the heart work harder.

Weight: Excess weight puts a strain on the entire circulatory system. It also makes people more likely to have other stroke risk factors such as high cholesterol, high blood pressure and diabetes.

The Five Most Common Stroke Symptoms Include:
- Sudden numbness or weakness of face, arm or leg, especially on one side of the body
- Sudden confusion, trouble speaking or understanding
- Sudden trouble seeing in one or both eyes
- Sudden trouble walking, dizziness, loss of balance or coordination
- Sudden severe headache with no known cause

Other Important but less Common Stroke Symptoms Include:
- Sudden nausea, fever and vomiting distinguished from a viral illness by the speed of onset (minutes or hours vs. several days)
- Brief loss of consciousness or period of decreased consciousness (fainting, confusion, convulsions or coma)

Brain Attack!
- Stroke is a "Brain Attack"
- Stroke happens in the brain rather than the heart.
- Stroke is an emergency!
- "Time is brain"

Source: National Stroke Association

Why Use the Term Brain Attack?
The origination of the term "brain attack" and its application to stroke are credited to Vladimir C. Hachinski, M.D., and John Norris, M.D., both world-renowned neurologists from Canada.

Stroke Prevention on Key Advice
A solution in the prevention of stroke can be found by the strengthening of blood vessels, making them more flexible and, in lowering the viscosity of the blood. This approach helps to prevent the rupture of cerebral blood vessels, while at the same time preventing blood platelets from clumping together in the formation of a clot.

Vitamin C and flavonoids found in many fruits and vegetables are known to improve the strength of blood vessels. Antioxidant nutrients again from fruit and vegetables further protect blood vessels by assault and damage from free radicals. Mosy importantly for stroke prevention the lowering of both cholesterol and blood pressure is vital. In the preceding sections I have detailed the profound benefits of flax seed oil and whole flax seed on lowering cholesterol and blood pressure. Recent research findings on the alpha-linolenic acid (ALA) Omega 3 in preventing stroke show those positive benefits.

Clinical Evidence
Study results reported in the May, 1995 issue of the American Heart Association's Stroke suggest that Omega 3 (alpha-linolenic acid) may protect against stroke. Analysing data from the long running Multiple Risk Factor Intervention Trail, researchers found that participants with high blood levels of alpha-linolenic acid (Omega-3) had nearly 40 percent lower risk of stroke, presumably because of the fatty acid's ability to reduce platelet "stickiness" and blood viscosity. Omega-3 fatty acids essentially prevent blood platelets from clumping together and forming a dangerous clot by making them "slippery".

Research from the Edinburgh Artery Study further confirms the role of Omega-3 in stroke prevention. In this study, more than 1,100 individuals were examined as part of a random sample survey of the general population of the Edinburgh area. Fatty acids were measured in groups with circulatory problems and those without apparent circulatory health problems. The level of alpha-linolenic acid "was significantly lower" in those persons who had suffered from strokes. Thus, conclude the researchers, "There may be some beneficial effects of the n-3 fatty acid, alpha-linolenic acid (omega 3)."

Experimental Research
Since we know that hardening of the arteries through excess fibrous tissue growth (sclerosis) is a cause of blockages, it would be good if we could reduce the progression of atherosclerosis, notes a researcher from the Department of Physiology, College of Medicine, University of Saskatchewan, Saskatoon, Canada. In this case, the beneficial effect of flaxseed is its powerful antioxidant properties, which defuses free radicals, implicated in the development of atherosclerosis.

In an experimental study, dietary flaxseed was given to animals on a high cholesterol diet likely to induce artery disease. Compared to animals not receiving flaxseed, the addition of this important source of Omega-3 fatty acids reduced the development of atherosclerosis by 46 percent. Based on the evidence, the researchers noted:

"Dietary flax seed supplementation could, therefore, prevent Hypercholesterolemia related heart attack and strokes."

Antioxidant Power
Purple grape juice also appears to have significant naturally occurring antioxidant power. Research findings suggests that diets rich in naturally occurring antioxidants may reduce the risk of heart disease (as well as some cancers). A recent study from the USDA (Department of Agriculture) found that Purple Grape juice has more than three fold the antioxidant power of such popular juices as apple, grapefruit, orange and tomato.

Grape Juice And Red Wine Theory
Prevention of stroke and the most important contributing factors to healthy cardiovascular function are:
- Flexibility of the arteries

- The speed at which LDL (the so-called "bad cholesterol") is oxidized
- Stickiness of blood.

Recently there has been much publicity on the positive effects of purple grape juice and red wine as having beneficial effects in possibly preventing some forms of cardiovascular illness. Whilst this may still be the case, Dr Ilker Durak's research at Ankara University indicates that there is little difference between grape juice, red and white wine as a possible cardiovascular aid.

Dr Durak *et al* research indicated: "That red wine, white wine and grape juice all have similarly high antioxidant potential to protect cellular structures against peroxidation reactions owing to their rich phenolic contents".

So keep on taking the grape juice, the red or white wine there appears to be some positive benefit.

Reference:

Comparison of Antioxidant Potentials of Red Wine, White Wine, Grape Juice and Alcohol,June 1999. Ilker Durak, Aslihan Avci, Murat Kaçmaz, Serap Büyükkoçak, M. Y. Burak Çimen, Serenay Elgün and H. Serdar Öztürk - Ankara University Medical Faculty, Department of Biochemistry, Ankara, Turkey

Omega-3 Protein Diet - An Aid To Preventing Heart Infarction and Stroke

Avoid:
Anything that contains hydrogenated oil or fat, these include: Margarines, Spreads Commercial Vegetable Oils, Salad Oils.
Processed Food that contain preservatives.
Non Foods such as refined sugars, sweetened jams, confectionary, orange juice in cartons (squeeze your own).
Pastries and Breads with refined flour or hydrogenated oils/fats from the bakers.
Pre-cooked meats, sausages and pates that contain preservatives.

In Moderation:
Animal fats such as lard, dripping and suet (fresh only).
Red meat and fresh meats should be organic or wild wherever possible.
Chocolate: only Belgium milk chocolate.
Dairy: Butter, Cheese.
Refer to 'Super Foods' section for some guide lines on what will give you that edge.

THE FIRST DAY ONLY

Start First Day In The Morning- Repeat At Midday and 6pm
- 5 tablespoons (80ml) of Flaxseed Oil mixed with 1 (15ml) tablespoon of honey and 1 glass of Purple Grape Juice **(Not For Diabetics)** or a glass of Champagne. Champagne has a positive benefit within this diet as it is easily absorbed. A little water to quench the thirst may be taken during this first day.

No Sugar: Purple Grape Juice or honey must be taken for sweetening in place of sugar (Not Diabetics).

A Beverage 3 Times Per Day: 1 cup Peppermint, Rose Hip or Black or Green tea is allowed before midday. These may be sweetened to taste with honey.

THE DIET PLAN SHOULD CONTINUE EACH DAY AS FOLLOWS:

BEFORE BREAKFAST – These kick start the digestion with good intestinal bacteria. 150ml (1 glass) of the following:
- Buttermilk, Acidophilus Milk or Kombucha Tea

1 Tbsp Apple Cider Vinegar in glass of water (Compulsory)

BREAKFAST – Breakfast should be light and wholesome. Fresh Fruit or Berries in Season, e.g. Blackberries, Cherries, Strawberries, Grated Apple. With a topping of Dessert Crème.
> Add 2 tablespoons of – Defatted Flax Flake or ground whole flaxseed to either a separate drink of choosing or to the Dessert Crème topping on the fruit. These are an important part of the diet.
> Beverage of Herbal Tea, Black Tea or Fresh Juice.

Or, **The Quick Fix Breakfast:** In a liquidiser add 100ml of water, one peeled and cored apple or pear, a handful of strawberries. Add two tablespoons of pre-ground flax seed or flaxseed flake and two tablespoons of flaxseed oil and 4 tablespoons of Yoghurt. Liquidise into a 'Smoothy' vary the fruit to your choice – Tastes great and is bursting with nutrition.

MID MORNING TEA (10AM) –
150ml (wine glass) of Kombucha Tea or a glass of pure fresh squeezed/juiced fruit juice

LUNCHEON

APPETISER
Small raw salad of choice - carrots, tomato, kohlrabi, grapes, celery or cauliflower. Horseradish, chives or parsley may be added for flavour. This may be as a salad on its own or combined as a wholemeal bread sandwich.

Before lunch take 1 tablespoon of Apple Cider Vinegar in a glass of water. This will aid digestion and is nutritionally beneficial

LUNCH – COOKED (optional)
Lunch can consist of home made chicken broth with vegetables and if available flaxseed bread. Add to broth, potatoes, buckwheat, barley or millet. Superb nutritional value.
You may add flavour to the broth with soy sauce or mixed herbs. Vary the type of vegetable, but always include some onion, tomato and carrot.
For a hearty meal, a baked jacket potato is always a favourite. By adding fresh chives, fresh parsley, caraway, or other herbs you will be increasing the nutritional value of your food. Only ever add parsley to a dish in the last 5 minutes of cooking.

DESSERT – (compulsory)
Some fresh fruit or berries, try to vary from those used for breakfast. Add and cover fruit with Dessert Crème or eat crème separate. Vary the Dessert Crème with vanilla refer to p170.

AFTERNOON (4PM) –
A small glass of organic red wine (no preservatives), purple grape juice or champagne with 1 heaped tablespoons of ground linseeds with honey to taste. Follow with (150ml) a glass of water.

AFTERNOON – 1 HOUR BEFORE SUPPER (5PM-6PM)
1 Tbsp of Apple Cider Vinegar in glass of water

EVENING MEAL/SUPPER –
This should be consumed no later than 7.30pm.
This may consist of:
Fish: Coldwater white fish such as cod, plaice, skate, halibut, sole or turbot. Avoid farmed reared salmon and trout.

Poultry: Chicken (without the skin), Rabbit, Turkey or wild game dish These should be grilled or baked. Refer to recipe and meal suggestions.

Beef or Lamb: (No more than 100g once per week) Grilled or casseroled. (remove all fat).
Include a jacket potato, pasta or rice with steamed green vegetables.

Quick supper:
An excellent nourishing supper is a homemade soup or broth with the chicken stock as the base. You may add Millet, Buckwheat or Oatmeal for extra nutrition.

Dessert:
A little fruit with a serving of Flax Dessert Crème refer to p170.

Fluid Intake: It is important to have no less than 2 litre of fluid per day. Taking into account fruit juices you will still need to have 8 glasses of water spread throughout the day. Avoid fluids 30 minutes either side of a meal as this will reduce the efficiency of digestive juices.
Purple Grape Juice: This has several beneficial effects, try to locate a good quality and drink two glasses per day. Purple grape juice has shown to increase Nitric Oxide (NO) by 70% in the body as well as having high anti-oxidant properties. Nitric Oxide dilates the blood vessels and has shown benefits with blood circulation to the extremities.

Preventing Osteoporosis

Calcium Is Not In The Right Place – The Bones

One of the most common causes of disability in women and especially with the onset of age is Osteoporosis or brittle bone disease. This illness frequently causes disfiguration, hospitalisation or surgery as a result of knocks or falls resulting in bone injury from fractures. Many women know that an adequate intake of calcium is essential for strong healthy bones. Some well informed individuals know that other minerals and nutrients such as glyconutrients, boron, magnesium and silicon together with vitamin D are essential to strong healthy bones. Just because the correct vitamins, minerals etc are supplemented, does not mean they get to where you want or need them. Our bodies need to function correctly to determine if the supplements get through to the bone, largely due to information sent from cell to cell, that is why the body must function correctly. What most individuals do not know is that there has been a large amount of research into osteoporosis disorders and the indicative findings have shown that that essential fatty acids (EFAs) may be notable bone protectors.

What appears to occur in some osteoporosis sufferers, is the body's storehouse of calcium become locked in other areas of the body, such as in tissues and organs adjacent to the bones, especially the kidneys and arteries, which left untreated will cause severe kidney disease and, more often, coronary artery disease (arteriosclerosis). Research has identified that EFA's (essential fatty acids), and in particular Omega-3 appears to be able to correct this anomaly of our aging bodies to store calcium in anywhere but the right places – The Bones.

Fortunately there is a great amount of research being carried out on the relationship and interaction between EFA's and calcium. The metabolic processing of calcium in our body's obviously requires much greater investigation since it appears it may offer a unique approach to not only the prevention of osteoporosis but also aid in preventing calcification of other vital organs that are associated with osteoporosis. With the numerous healing and therapeutic restoring benefits of EFA's they may well be the answer in preventing many chronic conditions and deaths related to disorders such as coronary artery blockages and kidney disease.

Omega-6 Fatty Acids
Linoleic acid (LA) is a fat (lipid) most commonly associated with cooking oils, typically corn oil, safflower oil and sunflower oil. "Many nutritional researchers speculate that while the Western diet is high in omega-6 fatty acids from vegetable oils, much of this fat is rendered unusable by over-refinement or hydrogenation," quote women's nutritional health expert Tori Hudson, N.D.
"Typically an excessive intake of these refined oils tend to elevate our body's inflammation levels and also interferes with the synthesis of other essential fatty acids".
Gamma-linolenic acid (GLA) is relatively scarce in the daily diet, but is essential in small amounts. GLA is derived from borage, black currant*, and evening primrose oils. Our body's requires dietary linoleic acid (omega-6) to make gamma-linolenic acid. However, often, its ability to do so is impaired because the body is not functioning properly due to the incorrect intake of dietary oils and fats. Therefore, most individuals may benefit from small supplements containing gamma-linolenic acid, in particular borage supplements.
*Black currant also contains an enzyme that is a GLA inhibitor.
Omega-3 fatty acids
Alpha-linolenic acid (omega-3) is the parent compound of the entire Omega-3 fatty acids family. Omega-3 is found in plant seeds, dark leafy green vegetables, hemp, nuts, whole grains, and but most abundantly in flax seed. Eicosapentaenoic acid (EPA), is found in concentrated in fish oils and walnuts and this very important EFA is also widely deficient in many individuals diet. EPA can be synthesized by the body naturally from alpha-linolenic acid found in flaxseed oil and flaxseed flake.

EFA-Osteoporosis Link

Research interest in EFA's and bone disease (osteoporosis) was highlighted from recent studies indicating essential fatty acid deficient animals developed chronic osteoporosis combined with elevated deposits of calcium in the animals kidneys and arteries, thereby suggesting that their body's metabolism and synthesis of this vital mineral is reduced without sufficient EFAs.

Drs. M. Kruger and D.F. Horrobin, at the Department of Physiology, University of Pretoria, South Africa noted. "This picture is similar to that seen in osteoporosis in the elderly, where the loss of bone calcium is associated with calcification of other tissues, particularly the arteries and the kidneys," Indeed, such ubiquitous calcium deposits in the body may foretell another way that essential fatty acids aid osteoporosis sufferers health, especially those of women.

Recent findings from mortality studies have indicated that the undesired calcification of bodily tissues adjacent to vital organs may be much more of a concern than the diagnosed osteoporosis itself, since the largest percentage of mortality in women suffering with osteoporosis are cardio vascular related especially those from blood clots and unrelated to fractures or other bone abnormalities. By keeping calcium in the bones exactly where it belongs, this may assist in preventing other common causes of death.

Dr. Kruger's final assessment. "The pilot controlled study suggests that GLA and EPA have beneficial effects on bone in this group of elderly patients, and that they are safe to administer for prolonged periods of time,"

How EFA's Aid Bone Health

According to scientific studies, essential fatty acids may:
- Likely to reduce urinary excretion of calcium.
- Increase the ability for calcium to be deposited back in the bone.
- Improvement in density and bone strength and the stimulation synthesis of thc bone collagen.

- Elevation of calcium absorption from the gut, due in part by enhancing the effects of vitamin D.

For women who may be concerned about their skeletal health, supplementing their diet with oils high in gamma-linolenic acid may improve absorption of calcium and enhance calcium content in the bone, while Omega-3 fatty acids may improve the blood levels of calcium and help to correct a deficient calcium effect in the bone. However, most bone mineral density studies done so far have used pure eicosapentaenoic acid (which is synthesized by the body from alpha-linolenic acid which can be found in flax or it may be taken directly with fish oil). Great care should be observed when supplementing with fish oils due to recent research from Greenpeace, which indicates the possibility of contamination from fish stocks due to polluted waters.

Omega-3 Protein Diet - An Aid For Osteoporosis
Avoid If Possible:
Anything that contains hydrogenated oil or fat, these include: Margarines, Spreads Commercial Vegetable Oils, Salad Oils.
Processed Food that contain preservatives.
Non Foods such as refined sugars, sweetened jams, confectionary, orange juice in cartons (squeeze your own).
From the bakers pastries and breads with refined flour or hydrogenated oils/fats
Pre-cooked meats, sausages and pates that contain preservatives.
In Moderation:
Animal fats such as lard, dripping and suet (fresh only).
Red meat and fresh meats should be organic or wild wherever possible.
Chocolate: only Belgium milk chocolate.
Dairy: Butter, Cheese.
Refer to 'Super Foods' section for some guide lines on what will give you that edge.

THE FIRST DAY ONLY

Start First Day In The Morning- Repeat At Midday and 6pm
- 5 tablespoons (80ml) of Flaxseed Oil mixed with 1 (15ml) tablespoon of honey and 1 glass of Purple Grape Juice **(Not For Diabetics)** or a glass of Champagne.
Champagne has a positive benefit within this diet as it is easily absorbed. A little water to quench the thirst may be taken during this first day.
- 1 Tbsp of Apple Cider Vinegar in glass of water

No Sugar: Purple Grape Juice or honey must be taken for sweetening in place of sugar (Not Diabetics).
A Beverage 3 Times Per Day: 1 cup Peppermint, Rose Hip or Black or Green tea is allowed before midday. These may be sweetened to taste with honey.

THE DIET PLAN SHOULD CONTINUE EACH DAY AS FOLLOWS:

BEFORE BREAKFAST –
1 tablespoons of Apple Cider Vinegar in a glass of water. If you are supplementing with calcium, mix calcium tablets/capsules in two tablespoons of cider vinegar and stir occasionally until fully dissolved may take up to 30 minutes,. Add some water and drink.

BREAKFAST – Breakfast should be light and wholesome. Fresh Fruit or Berries in Season, e.g. Blackberries, Cherries, Strawberries, Grated Apple. With a topping of Dessert Crème.
   Add 2 tablespoons of – Defatted Flax Flake or ground whole flaxseed to either a separate drink of choosing or to the Dessert Crème topping on the fruit. These are an important part of the diet.
   _ (half) Teaspoon of Organic Calcium Citrate *Refer to Glossary section for recipe.*
   Beverage of Herbal Tea, Black Tea or Fresh Juice.
Or, **The Quick Fix Breakfast:** In a liquidiser add 100ml of water, one peeled and cored apple or pear, a handful of strawberries. Add two tablespoons of pre-ground flax seed or flaxseed flake and two tablespoons of flaxseed oil and 4 tablespoons of Yoghurt or Quark. Liquidise into a 'Smoothy' vary the fruit to your choice – Tastes great and is bursting with nutrition.

LUNCHEON
APPETISER
Small raw salad of choice - carrots, tomato, kohlrabi, grapes, celery or cauliflower. Horseradish, chives or parsley may be added for flavour. This may be as a salad on its own or combined as a wholemeal bread sandwich.
Before lunch take 1 tablespoon of Apple Cider Vinegar in a glass of water. This will aid digestion and is nutritionally beneficial

LUNCH
Lunch can consist of home made chicken broth with vegetables and if available flaxseed bread. Add to broth, potatoes, buckwheat, barley or millet. Superb nutritional value.
You may add flavour to the broth with soy sauce or mixed herbs.
Vary the type of vegetable, but always include some onion, tomato and carrot.
For a hearty meal, a baked jacket potato is always a favourite. By adding fresh chives, fresh parsley, caraway, or other herbs you will be increasing the nutritional value of your food. Only ever add parsley to a dish in the last 5 minutes of cooking.

DESSERT
Some fresh fruit or berries, try to vary from those used for breakfast. Add and cover fruit with Dessert Crème or eat crème separate. Vary the Dessert Crème with vanilla refer p170.

AFTERNOON (4PM) –
A small glass of organic red wine (no preservatives), purple grape juice or champagne with 1 heaped tablespoons of ground linseeds with honey to taste. Follow with (150ml) a glass of water.

EVENING MEAL/SUPPER –
This should be consumed no later than 7.30pm. This may consist of:

Fish: Coldwater white fish such as cod, plaice, skate, halibut, sole or turbot. Avoid farmed reared salmon and trout.

Poultry: Chicken (without the skin), Rabbit, Turkey or wild game dish These should be grilled or baked. Refer to recipe and meal suggestions.

Beef or Lamb: Grilled or casseroled. (remove as much fat as possible).
Include a jacket potato, pasta or rice with steamed green vegetables.

Quick supper:
An excellent nourishing supper is a homemade soup or broth with the chicken stock as the base. You may add Millet, Buckwheat or Oatmeal for extra nutrition.

Dessert:
A little fruit with a serving of Flax Dessert Crème, refer p170.

Fluid Intake: It is important to have no less than 2 litre of fluid per day. Taking into account fruit juices you will still need to have 8 glasses of water spread throughout the day. Avoid fluids 30 minutes either side of a meal as this will reduce the efficiency of digestive juices.

For osteoporosis it is recommended that supplements of calcium, (calcium citrate *refer to glossary*), magnesium and boron be taken each day. Exercise in the form of weight bearing exercise aid with improving bone density.

Diabetes
'NHS is warned over soaring diabetes bill'
Daily Mail, June 11th 2001
Reported by Jenny Hope and James Chapman.

According to the figures, diabetes is running out of hand and becoming near epidemic proportions.

A recent report published by 'Diabetes UK' claims serious shortcomings in NHS care for diabetics. They estimate that within 10 years a fifth of the NHS budget, somewhere around £10 billion will be needed for the treatment of diabetes in the UK, and most of it can be avoided or substantially reduced with the correct diet and advance preventative action.

Diabetes is increasing due to several factors
- An ageing population
- A substantial rise in obesity
- Incorrect dietary habits

In general diabetes can be divided into two groups – Type 1 & 2.

• Type 1 (IDDM/insulin dependent diabetes mellitus). This is an autoimmune condition. That is the immune system, which exists to protect the body against infection and disease, turns against itself destroying the insulin-producing cells in the pancreas. This results in a complete deficiency of insulin.

• Type 2 (NIDDM/non insulin dependent diabetes). Caused either by a shortage of insulin or a fault in the way the body responds to insulin, known as insulin resistance. Insulin is produced but is unable to do its job of enabling the cells to absorb glucose from the blood.

Other types of diabetes

There are a number of other, less common, types of diabetes. They include:
- Gestational Diabetes, affects some women during pregnancy. It is often cleared up post delivery. Women

who have had GD during pregnancy are at a higher risk of developing diabetes in later life
- Maturity Onset Diabetes of the Young (MODY), an inherited rare form of diabetes in which there is impaired insulin secretion. The insulin action is normal or only mildly faulty.

Who Develops Diabetes?
Type 1: Diabetes is frequently diagnosed in children and young people below the age of 15, although it can occur at any age. Symptoms are often marked and diagnosis usually follows quickly.
Type 2: Diabetes mainly afflicts individuals from about the age of 40 years and onwards, which is why it used to be known as (MOD) Mature Onset Diabetes.
Several other risk factors include:
- Overweight.
- A close relative with diabetes,
- Of Asian or African-Caribbean origin
- Having gestational diabetes during pregnancy.
- Incorrect Diet

The symptoms of Type 2 diabetes are less marked with the result that it often goes undiagnosed for periods of up to 10 years. In fact, the onset of Type 2 occurs on average roughly between 9 and 12 years before sufferers are diagnosed, by which time over $1/3^{rd}$ and even up to half will already have signs of serious complications.

Diabetic Origins
The exact origins of diabetes are not yet fully understood. It is known that genetic, environmental and dietary factors may be involved, although the precise relationship between these has yet to be found. But I would have a little wager that good dietary nutrition plays a big role in avoiding the onset of age related diabetes.

Symptoms Of Diabetes
- Vision Blurred - causation abnormally high blood glucose levels changing the shape of the lens that affects focus.
- Increased thirst - causation increased urination
- Increased urination, especially at night – causation the body trying to rid itself of excess glucose.
- Weight loss-causation the body breaking down protein and fat stores as an alternative source of energy.
- Genital irritation – causation excess glucose irritating the genital area. Sometimes leads to the development of the yeast infection, thrush
- Extreme Tiredness – causation the reduction of energy as a result of the body being unable to transport glucose into the cells

Effects of diabetes
When the body is lacking in insulin it begins to break down fat reserves and muscle in an attempt to provide energy that is normally supplied by glucose. This metabolic anomaly can cause dramatic weight loss. With this condition, if fat and muscle is broken down the by-products called ketones form in the blood and the diabetic may lapse into a coma.

This comatose state is known as a Ketoacidotic coma and is more likely in Type 1 diabetics because they have an absolute shortage of insulin. Diabetics with Type 2 illness have less risk of ketoacidotic coma. However, unchecked and persistently high levels of blood glucose may cause damage to the body's blood vessels and nerves over a period of time leading to a number of extremely serious complications.

Is Diabetes Serious?
Contrary to popular opinion, diabetes is both progressive and life threatening with potentially devastating consequences for health. These include:
- High risk of cardiovascular/heart disease
- Stroke

- Kidney failure
- Diabetic Retinopathy - Eye disease leading to blindness
- Ulcerations of the foot/feet and sometimes amputation.

Research findings have shown the importance both of tight blood glucose control and of lowering blood pressure in delaying the onset or progression of complications. For this reason people with diabetes today may be prescribed other medications including anti-hypertensives, blood pressure lowering drugs, as well as blood glucose lowering medication or insulin.

Common Treatment For Diabetes
There are three types of treatment for diabetes - diet, tablets and/or insulin injections. The object of treatment is to bring the blood glucose levels back to a normal state thus preventing the onset of complications caused by persistently raised glucose levels.
As I mentioned earlier Type 2 diabetes is frequently referred to as non-insulin dependent diabetes, but some sufferers, an estimated 300,000 which is about 25 per cent of the diagnosed diabetics in the UK - do have to inject insulin. However, unlike diabetic patients with Type 1, they do not depend on it for their survival. For this reason their diabetes is described as insulin treated rather than insulin dependent.

Managing Diabetes
The old adage should have been written specifically for diabetes; *'An Ounce of Prevention Is Better Than A Pound of Cure'*, two out of every three people are dying needlessly from diabetic complications, which can be prevented or delayed. Many diabetics, as many as half, by the time they are diagnosed are already suffering with life threatening conditions. Findings from research have indicated that having fallen victim of diabetes the increase risk in dying prematurely from cardiovascular/heart disease doubles and may even treble once diabetes has developed.

Gone unchecked that's how serious it can be - **Dying prematurely.**

People suffering with diabetes must prepare themselves to take daily responsibility for their own health in order to stay well and avoid the onset of these chronic complications.

The prevention is relatively straight forward – Your Diet.

Supplements of Flaxseed Oil and Flax Flake together with GLA, which is derived from the oil of the Borage Seed will aid in bringing the glucose levels back to normal, aid in the correct cellular function in the body and help in protecting you from high blood pressure, cardiovascular disease, stroke, urinary and yeast infections.

If you are diagnosed with diabetes you will need to alter your diet, not substantially but just enough to control the condition.

Dietary Manipulation

It has been discovered recently that diabetics not only possess a dysfunction of their carbohydrate metabolism, but they also have a malfunction of their body's fat metabolism. This aspect of the illness has in the past, been largely ignored. This condition is of paramount importance, because with the majority of diabetic complications - heart disease, stroke neuropathy, retinopathy and impotence – they afflict the sufferer as a result of a faulty fatty acid metabolism, coupled with chronic hyperglycaemia.

Dietary manipulation has drawn much less attention, but by carefully establishing and restoring a balanced dietary fat intake combined with (Essential Fatty Acid) EFA oils it may be possible to restore optimal diabetic health. A review of past and present scientific literature underscores the importance of avoiding certain fats while supplementing other fatty acids to meet these ends.

What Should I Do?

The concerns of the charity Diabetes UK is that there is no national screening for diabetes and sufferers are not being diagnosed earlier enough. The answer - get along to your doctor, ask for a blood test to check on your sugar levels. It is in your hands.

Many of the new scientific nutritional discoveries are taking much too long to get through to the health care professionals. Some of the scientifically based new thinking and methods of approaching illness have been around and used to good effect for more than 10 years, yet as an example the American Diabetic Association's (ADA) approach is still antiquated and behind the times. Their policy on dietary fats is recommending a diet of which no more than 30% of daily calories are consumed as fat. This is way too high especially for someone suffering with diabetes. As scientific findings indicate as well as the more informed nutritionists suggest, a diet of no more than about 20% consumed as fats is nearer the mark, not only for diabetics but for everyone.

If as an example your total daily calorie intake was 2000 calories per day, then the proportion of the calories made up of fat should not be much more than 400 calories (2 tablespoon of flaxseed oil per day equals approximately 220 calories of fat).

Another important aspect to fat intake is that the incorrect type of fats have been proven to cause insulin insensitivity, whereby the cells in the body do not have the ability to allow blood sugar to enter the cell.

More specifically, the excess consumption of saturated fat and hydrogenated fats and oils contribute to insulin insensitivity.

Margarine is another hydrogenated fat laden product. It once stood on the pedestal as a possible benefit in controlling cardiovascular illness and was launched amidst a media fanfare as a replacement for butter with particular sections of the Food Industry marketing it by saying "Margarine is healthier for us than butter".

I'm afraid my reply to that is "RUBBISH". It was very likely margarine in the first place with its hydrogenated oils that brought about a significant increase in cardiovascular disease. Those earlier statements from some quarters of the food industry now know their marketing stance no longer stand up to scientific scrutiny.

A comment from a leading US nutritionist explained it quite simply with the reference. "There is only one possible way to describe hydrogenated oils, they are the most blatant example of biologically damaging substances being passed off as food".

It is known that both hydrogenated fats and saturated fats contribute to undesirable atherosclerotic plaque that hinders our circulation. Saturated fats in moderation can be burnt off with exercise. But, these unwanted, unhealthy oils and fats increase triglyceride and LDL (bad cholesterol) levels, which are major detriments to diabetic health. Research findings have identified hydrogenated and partially hydrogenated fats and oils can cause adverse effects to the nervous system of diabetics as well elevating the intracellular levels of Sorbitol, known to induce micro-vascular bleeding.

Benefits Of ALA (Omega 3) And GLA (Omega 6)

Dietary management has some tremendous benefits to the diabetic especially combined with a lowering of total fat consumption. Most diabetics with Type 2 conditions have brought about a metabolic change whereby they have rid themselves of pharmaceutical medications for their condition. Type I insulin dependant diabetics have also been able to reduce dosages of injected insulin, thus reducing the possibility of cardiovascular disease, which has been linked to insulin injection.

With what the biochemists and nutritionists have found over the last decade, is perhaps of greater importance and that is the role of beneficial fatty acids in the diet of diabetics. Cardiovascular complications that are attributed to diabetes have been reduced and often reversed with the inclusion of fatty acids as supplements.

It has been suggested in some quarters that there are studies suggesting strong evidence that confirms the benefits gained by including certain fatty acids in a diabetics diet and these have been 'buried'. Why would anyone want to hide this type of study if were true?

The answer is quite logical. The large pharmaceuticals corporations cannot patent naturally occurring nutrients, thus a study showing the benefits of a naturally occurring nutrient would deprive them of exorbitant pricing for diabetic medication.
Amongst the Omega family there is a fatty acid, gamma linolenic acid (GLA). Found in Borage seed oil, it is Mother Nature's most concentrated form at 23% gamma linolenic acid (GLA). The results of studies and the benefits of supplementing GLA in a diabetics diet are truly outstanding.

Supplementing with GLA has revealed:
- GLA normalised intercellular Sorbitol levels
- GLA increased HDL (good cholesterol) with a lower blood platelet aggregation.
- GLA reversed 'Diabetic Neuropathy' a painful and potentially serious condition.

Combining GLA and ALA (Omega 3) the following were evident from the studies:
- Reduces the risk of atherosclerosis
- Reduced triglycerides in blood
- Reduction of potent inflammatory mediators
- Enhances blood circulation
- Normalised glucose levels

The studies have revealed some interesting data as to how both GLA and Omega 3 work within the body of a diabetic. Findings from these studies reveal supplementing a diet with GLA has reported the normalisation of a malfunctioning fatty acid metabolism that is attributed to diabetes by circumventing the enzyme system responsible for this disorder. By using this round about route, the body's response to pain, swelling and inflammatory conditions, are stabilised. The arterial muscle tone that is responsible for blood pressure and optimal circulation may also be regulated by this system. With this type of overwhelming research and evidence noted here, a sensible approach may be to include the following;

- Reduce the consumption of saturated fats
- Remove from the diet all hydrogenated fats and oils
- Reduce the level of all fats to 20% of calories
- Supplement your diet daily with 1 teaspoon of Borage oil and 2 tablespoons of flaxseed oil to obtain both GLA and ALA fatty acids.

For Further Information Contact:
Diabetics UK – HELPLINE: 020 7323 1531

If there is some concern with a diabetic condition that is likely to cause serious health condition, the following Omega-3 Protein Diet may help you regain the helthfulness you desire.

Omega-3 Protein Diet - For The Diabetic

Prohibited:
Anything that contains hydrogenated oil or fat, these include: Margarines, Spreads Commercial Vegetable Oils, Salad Oils.
Processed Food that contain preservatives.
From the bakers breads with refined flour or hydrogenated oils/fats Cereals containing sugar. Cakes, biscuits and pastries with sugar related contents.
Pre-cooked meats, sausages and pates that contain preservatives.
Non Foods such as refined sugars, sweetened jams, confectionary.
All products containing sugar, glucose, glucose syrup, honey, dextrose, fructose etc.

Avoid:
Orange juice in cartons (squeeze your own).
Tea, coffee, alcohol, soft drinks, hot chocolate and Ovaltine.
Potatoes, ketchups, relishes, mustard and pre-packed sauces

THE FIRST DAY ONLY
Start First Day In The Morning- Repeat At Midday and 6pm
- 5 tablespoons (80ml) of Flaxseed Oil mixed with milk or yoghurt.
- 1 glass of Champagne. Champagne has a positive benefit within this diet as it is easily absorbed. A little water to quench the thirst may be taken during this first day.
- 1 Tbsp of Apple Cider Vinegar in glass of water

No Sugar – For sweetener use an Unsweetened Jam or Sugar Cane Molasses in cooking.
A Beverage 3 Times Per Day: 1 cup Peppermint, Rose Hip or Black or Green tea is allowed before midday.

THE DIET PLAN SHOULD CONTINUE EACH DAY AS FOLLOWS

BEFORE BREAKFAST – These kick start the digestion with good intestinal bacteria. 150ml (1 glass) of the following:
- Buttermilk, Acidophilus Milk

1 Tbsp of Apple Cider Vinegar in glass of water

BREAKFAST – Breakfast should be light and wholesome. Fresh Fruit or Berries in Season, e.g. Blackberries, Cherries, Grated Apple, Strawberries,. With a topping of Dessert Crème see p170.

Add 2 tablespoons of – Defatted Flax Flake or ground whole flaxseed to either a separate drink of choosing or to the Dessert Crème topping on the fruit. These are an important part of the diet. Include raw nuts, whole sunflower seeds, walnut, cashews,

Beverage of Herbal Tea, Black Tea or Fresh Juice.

Or, **The Quick Fix Breakfast:** In a liquidiser add 100ml of water, one peeled and core apple or pear, a handful of strawberries. Add two tablespoons of pre-ground flax seed or flaxseed flake and two tablespoons of flaxseed oil and 4 tablespoons or Yoghurt or Quark. Liquidise into a 'Smoothy' vary the fruit to your choice – Tastes great and is bursting with nutrition.

Watch your sugar level with fruit and root vegetable, choose those that are lower in natural sugar.

LUNCHEON

APPETISER
Small raw salad of choice - carrots, tomato, kohlrabi, grapes, celery or cauliflower. Horseradish, chives or parsley may be added for flavour. This may be as a salad on its own or combined as a wholemeal bread sandwich.

Before lunch take 1 tablespoon of Apple Cider Vinegar in a glass of water. This will aid digestion and is nutritionally beneficial

LUNCH – COOKED (optional)

Lunch can consist of home made chicken broth with vegetables and if available flaxseed bread. Add to broth, potatoes, buckwheat, barley or millet. Superb nutritional value.

You may add flavour to the broth with soy sauce or mixed herbs. Vary the type of vegetable, but always include some onion and carrot.

DESSERT – (compulsory)

Some fresh fruit or berries, try to vary from those used for breakfast. Add and cover fruit with Dessert Crème or eat crème separate. Vary the Dessert Crème with vanilla p170.

AFTERNOON (4PM) –

A small glass of organic red wine (no preservatives), champagne with 1 heaped tablespoons of ground linseeds with a little honey to taste. Follow with (150ml) a glass of water.

EVENING MEAL/SUPPER –

This should be consumed no later than 7.30pm. This may consist of:

Fish: Coldwater white fish such as cod, plaice, skate, halibut, sole or turbot. Avoid farmed reared salmon and trout.

Poultry: Chicken (without the skin), Rabbit, Turkey or wild game dish. These should be grilled or baked. *Refer to recipe and meal suggestions.*

Quick supper:
An excellent nourishing supper is a homemade soup or broth with the chicken stock as the base. You may add Millet, Buckwheat or Oatmeal for extra nutrition.

Dessert:
A little fruit with a serving of Flax Dessert Crème, p170.

Green Vegetable: Eat plenty of green vegetable, the darker the better.

Fluid Intake: It is important to have no less than 2 litre of fluid per day. Taking into account fruit juices you will still need to have 8 glasses of water spread throughout the day. Avoid fluids 30 minutes either side of a meal as this will reduce the efficiency of digestive juices.

After 30 days on this diet you can start by adding some of the 'avoid' list one by one and see if the glucose level in your blood stays the same. By introducing gradually you can ascertain which foods present a problem Do not introduce anything from the prohibitive list.

Explaining – The Omega-3 Protein Diet

The Omega-3 Protein Diet, flaxseed oil, defatted flake and flaxseed are not only for the chronically ill, but anyone wishing to improve their resistance to illness or reversal of minor ailments or for enhance well-being and optimising the immune system.
For those wishing to recovery from health issues, ailments and weight loss the diet plan is beneficial and essential.

The athlete looking for improved performance, energy and endurance plus a faster metabolic recovery following extreme exertion will benefit also from this diet.

The **Omega-3 Protein Diets** can be adapted to many different situations or illnesses. Research has identified in many cases that there are therapeutic advantages with this diet plan and for those wishing to sustain good health or as a positive preventative measure against chronic illness or improve athletic prowess the diet is ideal.

The restrictions on types of food apply to those diets for the chronically unwell. The object with these restrictions is to remove food bound inhibitors and toxins (preservatives, hydrogenated oils, trans fats etc), reduce saturated fats so that the flax seed oil may work much closer in harmony with the vital organs and improve the metabolic processes of the body.
Several benefits from using the diet may be felt within several days of starting, these repairs will continue throughout the body as the flaxseed oil works on every cell in the body.

How does flaxseed oil/Omega-3 work on every cell.
Simply, the combination of a sulphated protein (Quark, Cottage Cheese or Yoghurt) mixed with essential fatty acid omega-3 in the correct proportions allows the omega-3 to become water soluble allowing it to work on every cell in the body.

The normal **Omega-3 Protein Diets** requires the removal of all hydrogenated oils, contaminated processed foods, preservatives and non foods from your eating habits. It is best to consume fresh foods wherever possible. Fruit juices should be freshly squeezed if at all possible. A juicer for extracting the juice from vegetable and fruit is an excellent way of improving your nutritional intake. Chicken stock/broth is an important part of the diet.
You should be making up about 4 litres of stock each week.
Get used to reading food labels.

You do not want to be consuming foods that contain:

PRESERVATIVES AND PARTIALLY OR HYDROGENATED OIL OR FAT.

EAT FRESH WHEREVER POSSIBLE

There are some ingredients within the recipes that need to be explained so that the full benefits can be gained from the diet.

QUARK:
Quark is a pleasant tasting low cultured, non-fat dairy soft cheese. It is somewhat similar to cottage cheese. It is widely available from most supermarkets. Quark is mostly made in the Bavarian alpine region of Germany and is plentiful in sulphur-rich proteins which when combined with essential fatty acids as found in flax seed oil work together to rid the body of toxins and repair the body's tissue at a cellular level. Quark may be substituted with any good quality natural yoghurt, however, the combination level of oil and yoghurt are slightly different for those of Quark.
Within the recipes for the **Omega-3 Protein Diet** you will find some special base oil mixtures, dessert crème, muesli and mayonnaise base. These base mixes allow additional ingredients to be added so as to give a wide variety of tastes and flavours in the diet.

FLAX SEED OIL:
Flax seed oil contains a super rich form of essential fatty acids as well as being rich in lignans. Flax seed oil should be refrigerated to prevent rancidity.

Defatted Flax Flake or Whole Flaxseed
Take 2 tablespoons of fresh ground flaxseed or Flake each day. Either can be added to any cereal base, stew, soup or in your favourite beverage with a little honey or sugar free sweetening. Flax Flake should be stored in a cool place or in a refrigerator. Whole seed has up to 2 year shelf life at room temperature. You must ensure that you take 150ml of water or fluid for every one tablespoon of Ground Flaxseed or Flake.

FLAX/MAYONNAISE BASE:
The Flax/Mayo base can be adjusted to suit your own taste. The example will give you some idea for future mayonnaise base mixes. Mayo/Flax base mixes should be made at the time you want to use them. Mayonnaise bases should then be kept covered in a refrigerator until ready to use.
Ingredients and Preparation:
4 tablespoon Apple Cider Vinegar, 4 tablespoon of flaxseed oil, 125g of quark, 1 small gerkin or pickled cucumber. A little salt and fresh ground pepper to taste.
Combine all the ingredients in a blender and puree until smooth. Keep covered and refrigerated until ready to use.

BREAKFAST MUESLI BASE:
For those who enjoy Swiss style muesli breakfast the one detailed below is packed with high nutrition and fibre. This is optional but must not substitute the fresh fruit breakfast for the unwell. It may also be eaten at other times of the day if desired.
Gather together the ingredients and combine in a large bowl or on a clean worktop. Store in an airtight container until needed.
How to Prepare: Take _ to _ cup of muesli base and add to a deep side bowl. Add two heaped tablespoons of Ground Whole

flaxseed or Flake that has been liquidised for several seconds to a course consistency and add this to the muesli base mix. Add _ to _ cup of skimmed milk and 1 tablespoon of honey (to taste) to the muesli base and allow to soak for 5 minutes before consuming. Always add ground flaxseed at the time of consuming.
Ingredients:

400g	Rolled Oats	50g	Flaked Almonds
200g	Barley Oats	25g	Walnuts (Broken)
100g	Medium Oatmeal	50g	Hazelnut Kernels
100g	Millet Flakes	100g	Sultanas
50g	Buckwheat Flakes	100g	Raisin
50g	Pine Kernels	50g	Coconut, fine cut
50g	Sunflower Seeds		

FLAX/DESSERT CRÈME BASE:
This dessert crème is many peoples favourite. The sweetening can be of your choice but MUST NOT contain any refined sugar or conventional sugar laden jam. Ideally honey, pure grape juice or unsweetened jam.

In a separate bowl combine and mix well until the ingredients are of a creamy consistency. You may use a blender if necessary.

1 teaspoon	Local Honey (to taste)
4 tablespoons	Skimmed/Semi-skimmed milk or fruit juice
3 tablespoons	High Lignan Flax Seed Oil
100g	Quark or 125g Yoghurt.

Start with the oil and quark mix well together. Add the flavouring and a little milk or fruit juice, again mix well. Then add milk or fruit juice so you have the consistency you require.

You may also add vanilla, cinnamon or a flavour of your choice. Adjust the liquid consistency with additional fluid to taste.
It is important that you find a combination of flavour that you like.

Athletes, Sports Person Or Simply Energetic!

OMEGA 3 & 6 For Optimal Athletic Performance And Stamina.

- Increases Oxygen - Transporting throughout the body
- A Primary Energy Source for the Heart Muscle
- Reduction in Recovery Time from Strenuous Work Rate
- Regulates the Smooth Muscle and Autonomic Reflexes
- Aids and Stokes the Metabolic Rate
- Repairs muscle and body tissue faster

Flaxseed Oil and Flaxseed Flake have a tremendous beneficial effect on performance, stamina and recovery.

With professional sports persons and athletes - sports dietary plans are calculated on an individual (personal) basis in respect of training schedules, the amount of calories burnt during training and the requirement for weight gain and weight loss as well as specific times for the body to peak with fitness levels.
Dietary habit should not be set by the sport involved but on a personal basis.

Sports Nutrition As A Guide:
For protein intake guide levels refer to page 50.
- Carbohydrate: 60% - 65%
- Protein: Approximately 15%
- Fats: Approximately 20% - 25%

It is recommended for individuals who exercise on a near daily basis a diet should be comprised of 65-70% calories from carbohydrates, 15% of calories from protein and approximately 20% of calories from fat. A balanced diet will provide the essential fuels for training exercises and help maintain a favourable lipid (fat) profile. No evidence exists that performance can be improved by increasing dietary fat intake or by decreasing carbohydrate intake alone.

The body's utilization of carbohydrates and fats as fuels during exercise is dependent on the intensity, type and duration of the activity. It is generally found that carbohydrate use by the body increases with activity intensity and falls with extended duration of an activity. However, the amount of carbohydrate and fat used by muscles during exercise can be altered favourably, depending on fuel availability; the greater availability of fatty acids (Omega-3) increases fat use, and when more carbohydrates are available more carbohydrate is metabolised by the body for energy. This reciprocal interplay between fat and carbohydrate is where the benefits of flax seed oil play an important part of a sports diet.

If as an athlete you are looking for weight loss, then this should be done at a slow rate (1 kg per week) and if possible during the off-season. There exists substantial risks associated with rapid weight loss due to dehydration and food restriction include cardiovascular problems, fatigue, irritability, and long-lasting effects on body weight regulation.
Sports individuals who need to control body weight by restricting fluid or dietary intake will benefit from a pre-exercise meal having a high carbohydrate content.

Sports individuals and athletes should be able to urinate before and after they train or compete. If they are unable to do so, it is possible not enough fluid has consumed. Dehydration due to exercise and high temperature can lead to body disorders such as heat cramps to life-threatening heat stroke. Sports persons and athletes in the field during the hotter summer months need to consume a carbohydrate-electrolyte drink during and after matches.

Drinking fluids has an influence on the reduction of the increase in body temperature (hyperthermia) and the amount of stress on the cardiovascular system, especially when exercising in hot environments (Coyle & Montain, 1993).

To gain lean body mass is dependent on training and exercise status. In an individual who does not exercise, a gain in lean body mass in a one-year period might be up to 20%, whereas gains in active/trained athletes are much slower. Exercise and training schedules that incorporate principles of intensity, overload, progression, recovery between training sessions in combination with adequate energy and protein intake (refer page 48) create a favourable condition for muscle and strength improvement.

In distance running, there is evidence that the number of injuries sustained by runners, as well as the extent of muscle damage, is greater in individuals who train and exercise with low muscle glycogen. The consumption of adequate with a high carbohydrate content is important to help elevate blood glucose levels and diminish the extent of dehydration.

Athletic performance is governed with the body's availability of carbohydrate store (glucose, muscle glycogen and liver glycogen) all of which play a critical role. Individuals who train and exercise on successive days must consume adequate carbohydrate and energy to reduce the likelihood of fatigue associated with the cumulative onset of muscle glycogen depletion. Glycogen depletion can occur during training schedules in sports that involve intermittent efforts, but care in dietary choice can avoid this. Pay particular attention to food consumed from fast food outlets.

Omega-3 Protein Diet® - Athletically Fit and Well

Try To Avoid If Possible:
Anything that contains hydrogenated oil or fat, these include: Margarines, Spreads Commercial Vegetable Oils, Salad Oils. Processed Food that contain preservatives. Non Foods such as refined sugars, sweetened jams, confectionary, orange juice in cartons (squeeze your own).
Pastries and Breads with refined flour or hydrogenated oils/fats from the bakers.
Pre-cooked meats, sausages and pates that contain preservatives.

In Moderation:
Animal fats such as lard, dripping and suet (fresh only).
Red meat and fresh meats should be organic or wild wherever possible.
Chocolate: only Belgium milk chocolate.
Dairy: Butter, Cheese.
Refer to 'Super Foods' section for some guide lines on what will give you that edge.

THE FIRST DAY ONLY

The diet should start when you have at least one rest day between training schedules.

Start First Day In The Morning- Repeat At Midday and 6pm
- 5 tablespoons (80ml) of Flaxseed Oil mixed with
- 1 (15ml) tablespoon of honey and
- 1 tablespoon of ground flax seed
- 1 glass of fresh pressed fruit juice **(Not For Diabetics)**

No Sugar: Fruit Juice or honey must be taken for sweetening in place of sugar (Not Diabetics).

A Beverage 3 Times Per Day: These may be sweetened to taste with honey. Maintain normal fluid intake.

The diet should be adjusted around the individual athlete then consideration for the level of exercise or training schedule.
THE DIET PLAN SHOULD CONTINUE

EACH DAY AS FOLLOWS:

BEFORE BREAKFAST – These kick start the digestion with good intestinal bacteria. 150ml (1 glass) of either of the following: Buttermilk, Acidophilus Milk or
1 tablespoon of Apple Cider Vinegar in water.

BREAKFAST – Breakfast should be light and wholesome. Fresh Fruit or Berries in Season, e.g. Blackberries, Cherries, Grated Apple, Strawberries include a topping of Dessert Crème.

> Add 2 tablespoons of – Defatted Flax Flake or ground whole flaxseed to either a separate drink of choosing or to the Dessert Crème topping on the fruit. These are an important part of the diet. Beverage of Fresh Juice.

Or, **The Quick Fix Breakfast:** In a liquidiser add 100ml of water, one peeled apple or pear a handful of strawberries. Add two tablespoons of pre-ground flax seed or flaxseed flake and two tablespoons of high lignan flax seed oil and 4 tablespoons of Yoghurt or Quark. Liquidise into a 'Smoothie' vary the fruit to your choice – Tastes great and is bursting with nutrition.

MID MORNING TEA (10AM) –
150ml (wine glass) glass of pure fresh squeezed/juiced fruit juice plus carbohydrates depending on time of exercise.

LUNCHEON
APPETISER
Small raw salad of choice - carrots, tomato, kohlrabi, grapes, celery or cauliflower. Horseradish, chives or parsley may be added for flavour. This may be as a salad on its own or combined as a wholemeal bread sandwich.
Before lunch take 1 tablespoon of Apple Cider Vinegar in a glass of water. This will aid digestion and is nutritionally beneficial

LUNCH
Lunch can consist of home made chicken broth with vegetables and if available flaxseed bread. Add to broth, potatoes, buckwheat, barley or millet. Superb nutritional value.

You may add flavour to the broth with soy sauce or mixed herbs. Vary the type of vegetable, but always include some onion and carrot. For a heartier meal, a baked jacket potato is always a favourite. By adding fresh chives, fresh parsley, caraway, or other herbs you will be increasing the nutritional value of your food. Only ever add parsley to a dish in the last 5 minutes of cooking.

DESSERT

Some fresh fruit or berries, try to vary from those used for breakfast. Add and cover fruit with Dessert Crème or eat crème separate. Vary the Dessert Crème with vanilla.

AFTERNOON (4PM) –

Fruit juice with 1 heaped tablespoons of ground flax seeds with honey to taste. Follow with (150ml) a glass of water.

EVENING MEAL/SUPPER –

This should be consumed no later than 7.30pm. This may consist of:

Fish: Coldwater white fish such as cod, plaice, skate, halibut, sole or turbot.
Avoid farmed reared salmon and trout.

Poultry: Chicken (without the skin), Rabbit, Turkey or wild game dish These should be grilled or baked. Refer to recipe and meal suggestions.

Beef or Lamb: Grilled or casseroled. (remove as much fat as possible).

Include a jacket potato, pasta or rice with steamed green vegetables.

Quick supper:

An excellent nourishing supper is a homemade soup or broth with the chicken stock as the base. You may add Millet, Buckwheat or Oatmeal for extra nutrition.

Dessert:

A little fruit with a serving of Flax Dessert Crème.

Fluid Intake: It is important to drink adequate liquids to allow for exercise and training. Avoid fluids 30 minutes either side of a meal as this will reduce the efficiency of digestive juices.

Purple Grape Juice: This has several beneficial effects, try to locate a good quality and drink two glasses per day. Purple grape juice has shown to increase Nitric Oxide (NO) by 70% in the body as well as having high anti-oxidant properties. Nitric Oxide dilates the blood vessels and has shown benefits with blood circulation to the extremities.

For The Athlete: You will need to consume no less than four tablespoons of flaxseed oil each day plus three tablespoons of ground whole flaxseed

Pregnancy and Omega 3

The first pregnancy-related need for Polyunsaturated Fatty Acids, which includes both omega-6 and omega-3 occurs up to and during the 90 days prior to conception. This is a critical time for cell respiration and commitment, and the cell division requires ARA and DHA (docosahexaenoic acid) both components synthesized by the body from omega-3, which facilitates growth and development of the foetus. There is now sufficient evidence that by including within your daily diet omega-3 sourced from flaxseed, during pregnancy, is likely to prevent pregnancy-induced hypertension, assists in prolonging gestation, a likelihood of increased birth weight and reduces the incidence of premature birth. Recent data support the view that the intake of DHA (omega-3) during pregnancy should be in the amount of at least one tablespoon of flaxseed oil per day.

Fetal stage

DHA is an important contribution for optimal nervous system development. EPA another by product of omega-3 synthesized by the body plays an important part in the foetal brain development. It must be remembered that, to achieve these synthesises you should not have excessive saturated fats in the body. Eat saturated fats in moderation - do not go to a low fat diet.
During the last trimester of pregnancy (90 days), when the foetal demand for neurological and vascular growth is greatest, there is an elevated growth of DHA in the liver and brain of the foetus. A mothers diet high in DHA will greatly enrich the DHA concentration in the blood of the newborn infant.

Pre-eclampsia

Blood fats (lipids), triglycerides and cholesterol may increase several folds during pregnancy. It is not unusual for a slight increase in blood pressure. The risk of developing pre-eclampsia and the onset of subsequent premature birth is increased if these, otherwise normal changes are increased above certain levels.
Severe forms of pregnancy-induced hypertension have been found to be beneficially mediated by omega-3 fatty acids (Secher et al, 1991).

In light of their very strong hypo-triglyceridemic and hypotensive effects, omega-3 fatty acids along with other nutritional factors, may be significant for the prevention of pre-eclampsia.

The mother's blood pressure responses depend on the ARA/EPA ratio in the vessel wall. EPA will benefit the mother's heart and circulation, and DHA will definitely be good for the development of foetal brain and nervous system.

DHA and EPA are naturally synthesized by the body from their parent fatty acid omega-3. The richest source of omega-3 is flaxseed and flaxseed oil. As additional aid, wild red salmon or walnuts are an excellent source of EPA.

The only fats to consume during pregnancy are butter in moderation, pure unrefined virgin olive oil and pure coconut oil.

If you're not a fish eater, you could take a supplement. Do make sure you choose a supplement formulated specially for pregnant women, though, as some fish oil supplements, such as cod liver oil, may contain high levels of retinol (the animal form of vitamin A), which can cause birth defects if taken in large amounts during early pregnancy.

Always check product labels carefully and ask your midwife or consultant if you are concerned.

At present, there is no recommended daily intake of omega 3 fatty acids, although there is currently research in progress that will determine the RDA. In the meantime, eat a varied range of foods, including some fresh oily fish, fresh vegetables, a tablespoon of the freshest flaxseed oil and look forward to a lovely bouncing baby.

Breakfast For The Young

"A full stomach doesn't like to study!" according to an old Latin saying. Children at the beginning of the day need a breakfast that is energy packed and is easy to digest.

With this for breakfast they'll last through to lunch-time.

Why!

If children or anyone for that matter eat a breakfast that is fat laden and heavy with refined food, then their concentration will diminish, performance impaired for studying or their mental activity is reduced.

The moment food is difficult to digest, the brain has to send messages to the digestive processes initially rather than get on with the process of learning or studying.

The basic breakfast should start with:
- 2 Tbsp Fresh Ground Flaxseed or Flaxseed Flake
- 1 Tbsp Lignan Rich Flaxseed Oil
- 60g Quark or 100g Yoghurt
- 1 Teaspoon Honey to taste
- 4 Tbsp favourite fruit juice (or to taste)

Additions: You may wish to add different fruits, berries, walnut or seeds.

If children dislike the Quark or Yoghurt then mix the ground flaxseed or flake with a traditional breakfast cereal using semi-skimmed milk.

Stock Making

By Sally Fallon – Weston A. Price Foundation
Author of: 'Nourishing Traditions: The Cookbook that Challenges Politically Correct Nutrition' and the Diet Dictocrats with Mary G. Enig, PhD.

Science validates what our grandmothers knew. Rich homemade chicken broths help cure colds. Stock contains minerals in a form the body can absorb easily—not just calcium but also magnesium, phosphorus, silicon, sulphur and trace minerals. It contains the broken down material from cartilage and tendons--stuff like chondroitin sulphates and glucosamine, now sold as expensive supplements for arthritis and joint pain.

Fish stock, according to traditional lore, helps boys grow up into strong men, makes childbirth easy and cures fatigue. "Fish broth will cure anything," is another South American proverb. Broth and soup made with fish heads and carcasses provide iodine and thyroid-strengthening substances.

When broth is cooled, it congeals due to the presence of gelatine. The use of gelatine as a therapeutic agent goes back to the ancient Chinese. Gelatine was probably the first functional food, dating from the invention of the "digester" by the Frenchman Papin in 1682. Papin's digester consisted of an apparatus for cooking bones or meat with steam to extract the gelatine. Just as vitamins occupy the centre of the stage in nutritional investigations today, so two hundred years ago gelatine held a position in the forefront of food research. Particularly the French, who were seeking ways to feed their armies and vast numbers of homeless in Paris and other cities, universally acclaimed gelatine as a most nutritious foodstuff. Although gelatine is not a complete protein, containing only the amino acids Arginine and glycine in large amounts, it acts as a protein sparer, helping the poor stretch a few morsels of meat into a complete meal. During the siege of Paris, when vegetables and meat were scarce, a doctor named Guerard put his patients on gelatine bouillon with some added fat and they survived in good health.

The French were the leaders in gelatine research, which continued up to the 1950s. Gelatine was found to be useful in the treatment of a long list of diseases including peptic ulcers, tuberculosis, diabetes, muscle diseases, infectious diseases, jaundice and cancer. Babies had fewer digestive problems when gelatine was added to their milk. The American researcher Francis Pottenger pointed out that, as gelatine is a hydrophilic colloid, which means that it attracts and holds liquids, it facilitates digestion by attracting digestive juices to food in the gut. Even the epicures recognized that broth-based soup did more than please the taste buds. "Soup is a healthy, light, nourishing food" said Brillant-Savarin, "good for all of humanity; it pleases the stomach, stimulates the appetite and prepares the digestion."

ATTENTION TO DETAIL

Stock or broth begins with bones, some pieces of meat and fat, vegetables and good water. For beef and lamb broth, the meat is browned in a hot oven to form compounds that give flavour and colour--the result of a fusion of amino acids with sugars, called the Maillard reaction. Then all goes in the pot--meat, bones, vegetables and water. The water should be cold, because slow heating helps bring out flavours. Add vinegar to the broth to help extract calcium--remember those egg shells you soaked in vinegar until they turned rubbery.

Heat the broth slowly and once the boil begins, reduce heat to its lowest point, so the broth just barely simmers. Scum will rise to the surface. This is a different kind of colloid, one in which larger molecules--impurities, alkaloids, large proteins called lectins--are distributed through a liquid. One of the basic principles of the culinary art is that this effluvium should be carefully removed with a spoon. Otherwise the broth will be ruined by strange flavours. Besides, the stuff looks terrible. "Always Skim" is the first commandment of good cooks.

Two hours simmering is enough to extract flavours and gelatine from fish broth. Larger animals take longer- 4 to 6 hours for stock made from chicken, turkey or duck and overnight for beef broth. Broth should then be strained. Perfectionists will want to chill the broth to remove the fat. Stock will keep several days in the refrigerator or may be frozen in plastic containers. Boiled down it concentrates and becomes a jellylike fume or demi-glaze that can be reconstituted into a sauce by adding water.

CUTTING CORNERS

Research on gelatine came to an end in the 1950s because the food companies discovered how to induce Maillard reactions and produce meat-like flavours in the laboratory. In a General Foods Company report issued in 1947, chemists predicted that almost all natural flavours would soon be chemically synthesized. And following the Second World War, food companies also discovered monosodium glutamate (MSG), a food ingredient the Japanese had invented in 1908 to enhance food flavours, including meat-like flavours. Humans actually have receptors on the tongue for glutamate. It is the protein in food that the human body recognizes as meat.

Any protein can be hydrolysed to produce a base containing free glutamic acid or MSG. When the industry learned how to make the flavour of meat in the laboratory, using inexpensive proteins from grains and legumes, the door was opened to a flood of new products including bouillon cubes, dehydrated soup mixes, sauce mixes, TV dinners and condiments with a meaty taste.

"Homemade" soup in most restaurants begins with a powdered soup base that comes in a package or can and almost all canned soups and stews contain MSG, often found in ingredients called hydrolysed proteins. The fast food industry could not exist without MSG and artificial meat flavours to make "secret" sauces and spice mixes that beguile the consumer into eating bland and tasteless food.

Short cuts mean big profits for producers but the consumer is short changed. When homemade stocks were pushed out by cheap substitutes, an important source of minerals disappeared from the modern diet. The thickening effects of gelatine could be mimicked with emulsifiers but the health benefits were lost. Most serious, however, were the problems posed by MSG, problems the industry has worked very hard to conceal from the public. In 1957, scientists found that mice became blind and obese when MSG was administered by feeding tube. In 1969, MSG-induced lesions were found in the hypothalamus region of the brain. Other studies all point in the same direction--MSG is a

neurotoxic substance that causes a wide range of reactions, from temporary headaches to permanent brain damage.
Why do consumers react to factory-produced MSG and not to naturally occurring glutamic acid found in food? One theory is that the glutamic acid produced by hydrolysis in factories contains many isomers in the right-handed form, whereas natural glutamic acid in meat and meat broths contains only the left-handed form. L-glutamic acid is a precursor to neurotransmitters, but the synthetic form, d-glutamic acid, may stimulate the nervous system in pathological ways.

Stock, Broth And Soup Making

To make the perfect stocks or sauces:
- Use only heavy based pans, preferable cast iron, but stainless steel will do.

- Choose bones that best suit the meat presented: Beef for beef or Lamb for lamb etc.
- Ideally break/crack large bones with a hammer so as to get liquid into centre of the bone.
- All ingredients must be clean and sound, no mould or rancid fat.
- To sterilize, wash thoroughly first then plunge bones in boiling water for 2-3 minutes before going into stockpot.
- Add 1 or 2 tablespoons of cider vinegar or white wine vinegar to stock water.
- Start stock from cold water and bring to a gentle rolling boil. Turn heat down so that water is just simmering.
- Always cook bones and meat for at least 4 hours before adding the vegetables.
- Simmer bones in stockpot until surface is pitted with small holes. A richer flavoured can be obtained if roasted before simmering.
- **Do not** cook vegetable for too long during the cooking process or leave them in the stock to cool down. Once the vegetables are cooked they will start to absorb the flavour from the bones.
- Do not cook fish stock for more than 45 minutes.
- Do not use too many green vegetable – they can make the stock bitter.
- Use herbs and spices very sparingly - this can also give a stock a bitter taste.
- Starchy ingredients, such as potato will make stock cloudy and may also give a sour taste.
- Remove white scum that comes to the top. Do not remove brown scum, as this is highly nutritious protein that has set in the liquid.
- As soon as the stock has cooked, remove ingredients and store in an ovenproof glass dish uncovered. Cool and remove fat then refrigerate.
- For thickening use a slate of corn flour or ordinary milled flour.

- For a stronger flavour reduce stock on a fast heat.
- Never store stock in any type of metal pan as this can give the stock a sour taste. Always use glass or plastic.
- Never salt stock before storage; adjust to your taste when the stock is to be finally used. Freezing or long storage increases the taste of salt.
- **There is eight times the nutritional value from the gelatine in bones than there is from the gelatine contained in the meat flesh.**

Sauce/Gravy

The first step is to "deglaze" coagulated pan juices in the roasting pan by adding 150ml (1 cup) red or white wine. Add tablespoon of white flour, bringing to a boil and stirring with a wooden spoon to loosen.

Then add 600ml (4 cups) of home made stock, bring to a boil. (Use chicken stock for chicken dishes, beef stock for beef dishes, etc.). Allow gravy/sauce to boil vigorously, uncovered, until desired thickness is achieved.

If sauce becomes too thick, thin with a little water.

The final step in sauce making is to taste and add sea salt if necessary.

Storing Stocks

Most stocks can be stored for up to 1 week in a refrigerator. Make sure the stock is covered. Stocks may also be deep frozen for many months. When deep freezing stocks reduce the amount of salt that is added when cooking the stock. The flavour of salt will increase through freezing. When using stored stocks they must be brought back to the boil for 10 minutes before serving.

Remove Any Fat

Ensure all fat is removed before using a stock in any recipe. If you do not intend storing a stock in a refrigerator or freezer, the stock must be made several hours before use. If you intend to use a stock the same day as preparing the recipe allow the stock to cool so that any fat may rise to the top. If you do not have time to refrigerate, take some kitchen towel pieces and draw the paper towel across the surface of the stock. You will have to do this several times so that the paper towel to absorb most of the fat on the surface.

Soup Serving
It is important to choose a soup that compliments the main course. Your guests will appreciate a little variety in a meal.
If you have a heavy pie main course do not serve a hearty broth type soup before hand, preferably a lighter soup would suit a heavy main course. The reverse is the case with a light main course a more substantial soup than the main course should be served.
Do not serve a fish soup before a fish main course or a vegetable soup such as tomato soup before a main course that is heavily flavoured with tomatoes or tomato sauce.

Basic Stock:
Ingredients can be varied depending on what is available. Keep the proportion of 450 gm (1lb) of solid ingredients to 1.5 litre of liquid. This will make about 1.0 litre of stock.

Ingredients:
1kg of bones and meat (beef, chicken, lamb, veal or fish)
3 litre clean water
1 teaspoon of Pure Sea Salt
2 large carrots. Scrubbed, peeled and cut into large pieces.
1 large onion, peeled and halved
2 sticks of celery washed thoroughly, cut into large pieces.
2 Tablespoon of Apple Cider Vinegar or White wine Vinegar

Break or crack bones with hammer if they are large. For a slightly darker and improved flavour roast bones for 30 minutes in a hot oven. Cut meat into large pieces and place meat and bones in a

heavy pan of cold salted water. Add vinegar. If you intend to freeze the stock do not add salt.
Bring slowly to the boil and turn heat down so that the water is just moving on the surface. Remove any white scum formed on the top.
Cover with well fitting lid and simmer gently for 4 hours. Then add carrots, onion and celery, cover again and simmer for a further 2 hours or until the vegetables are soft - do not allow vegetable to break up.
Strain through a nylon or hair sieve and discard solids.
Check taste and if the stock lacks a little flavour boil rapidly to reduce its volume and concentrate the flavour. Allow to cool, removing any fat on surface. Use within 2 or 3 days if kept in refrigerator or divide into smaller quantities and deep freeze for later use.

Chicken Stock
1 Whole free-range chicken or 1kg of bony chicken parts, such as legs and wings
3 Litres cold water with 2 tablespoons Apple Cider Vinegar.
1 large onion, coarsely chopped
2 carrots, peeled and coarsely chopped
2 celery stalks, coarsely chopped
1 bunch parsley.
Note: Organic farm-raised, free-range chickens give the best results.

Remove breast from chicken and reserve for another dish. If you are using a whole chicken, remove the neck, fat glands and the gizzards from the cavity. Cut chicken parts into several pieces. Place chicken or chicken pieces in a large stainless steel pot with water, vinegar and all vegetables except parsley. Allow to stand for 30 minutes to 1 hour. Bring to a boil, and remove scum that rises to the top. Reduce heat, cover and simmer for 5 to 6 hours. The longer you cook the stock, the richer and more flavourful it

will be. About 10 minutes before finishing the stock, add parsley. This will impart additional mineral ions to the broth.
Remove whole chicken or pieces with a slotted spoon. If you are using a whole chicken, allow to cool, removing chicken meat from the carcass. Reserve for other uses, such as salads, sandwiches or curries. Strain the stock into a large bowl and when cooled reserve in your refrigerator until the fat rises to the top and congeals. Skim off this fat and reserve the stock in covered containers in your refrigerator or freezer.

Beef Stock
1kg Beef marrow and knuckle bones
2 litre cold water
3 Tablespoons of Apple cider vinegar
3 Onions, coarsely chopped; 3 Carrots, coarsely chopped;
3 Celery stalks, coarsely chopped
6 black peppercorns, 1 bunch parsley

Place the knuckle and marrowbones in a very large pot with vinegar and cover with water. Let stand for one hour. Meanwhile, place the meaty bones in a roasting pan and brown at 350• in the oven. When well browned, add to the pot along with the vegetables. Pour the fat out of the roasting pan, add cold water to the pan, set over a high flame and bring to a boil, stirring with a wooden spoon to loosen up coagulated juices. Add this liquid to the pot. Add additional water, if necessary, to cover the bones; but the liquid should come no higher than within one inch of the rim of the pot, as the volume expands slightly during cooking. Bring to a boil. A large amount of scum will come to the top, and it is important to remove this with a spoon. After you have skimmed, reduce heat and then add the thyme and crushed peppercorns.
Simmer stock for 12 hours. Just before finishing, add the parsley and simmer another 10 minutes. After straining you will have a delicious and nourishing clear broth that forms the basis for many wonderful recipes. Remove bones with a slotted spoon. Strain the stock into a large bowl. Allow to cool in the refrigerator and

remove the congealed fat that rises to the top. Transfer to smaller containers and to the freezer for long-term storage.

Vegetable Stock:
Use relatively large pieces of fresh vegetable and the liquid in which rice or pasta has been cooked. Use within 48 hours unless DEEP FROZEN. Dry roasting vegetables in a hot oven will produce a slightly darker colour.

White Stock:
Used as basis for white cream sauces in chicken, rabbit or veal dishes. Use also in gelatines and in dishes that require jellied stock.

Meat Glazes
Brown meat stock can be made into a delicious glaze for both cold and hot meats. Measure 300 ml of stock, from which, remove every piece of fat; this is best achieved by having chilled the stock for several hours in the refrigerator. Pour stock into a heavy based saucepan and boil rapidly with no lid. Skim off any scum that rises and forms on the surface. Continue to boil the stock until it reaches the consistency of thick treacle. Make sure you stir the stock continuously to prevent burning. When it has reached the desired consistency, remove from the heat and allow it to cool before spooning over the meat. This glaze can also be kept for up to a week in a refrigerator.

Fish Stock:
Do not use oily fish.
Ideally Plaice, Cod, Coley and most deep sea white fish.
3 fish whole carcasses with bone and heads.
2 tablespoons extra virgin olive oil; small knob of butter
2 onions, peeled and quartered chopped; 1 carrot, peeled and coarsely chopped
1 sprig of parsley; 1 sprig of thyme; 1 bay leaf

1/2 cup dry white wine or vermouth; 50 ml white wine vinegar
1 _ litre Clean water.

If you wish to make a seafood sauce then replace half of the fish carcasses with the same quantity by weight of peeled prawn shells.
The better quality of the fish carcass the better the stock.

Be sure to use the heads as well as the body—these are especially rich in iodine and fat-soluble vitamins. Classic cooking texts advise against using oily fish such as salmon for making broth, probably because highly unsaturated fish oils become rancid during the long cooking process.
Using two pans. In the first add the water and fish carcasses and bring slowly to the boil. In the second pan melt the Olive Oil with small knob of unsalted butter. Add the vegetables to the second pan and cook very gently for 30 minutes or until the vegetables are soft. Add the wine to the second pan and bring to the boil. Transfer the fish carcasses to the second pan and add to the vegetables. Add the white wine vinegar. Bring to a boil and skim off the scum and add the herbs. Lower the heat and cover. Simmer stock gently for 45 minutes. Remove carcasses with slotted spoon and strain the liquid with hair sieve or nylon. Cool and refrigerator or deep freeze. Chill well in the refrigerator and remove any congealed fat before transferring to the freezer for long-term storage.

Food & Kitchen Basics

Foods To Avoid:
The following list constitutes foods that, someone who is chronically ill should not consume. However the odd mad moment does have some positive psychological role in maintaining good health, choose those moments and the food well!

Those that are well would be advised to reduce their consumption of any of the foods shown on the list.

It is important to plan what you want to eat a day or so in advance, look forward to a good meal. Enjoy your food, don't become a slave to food – invent new recipes that you will enjoy. Bon Appetite!

Processed food that contain hydrogenated oil or partially hydrogenated oil.
Animal fat, suet, dripping
All processed and cured meats that contain preservatives
Processed fats, margarines, vegetable fats, lard and mayonnaise s
Foods containing artificial colours, preservatives or additives.
Refined sugars and related products and cereals containing sugar
Sugar laden jams, preserves, treacle, confectionary, chocolate, and crisps.
Refined flours and related products
Pastries, pies and biscuits
Alcohol (except organic red wine/white wine or champagne)
Burnt, Charred, Rancid and Stale foods
Stale foods such as grains, pulses and nuts with mould evident.
Reduce fried foods

Do not use microwave ovens – Bake, grill, boil or casserole

What We Can Eat
Eat natural and fresh foods wherever possible
Eat 'wild' meat or organic meat in preference
Use butter in place of spreads, but don't go mad with the butter.
Eat more raw foods – fruits, vegetables
Juice as much food as possible
Build up a stock of pulses, legumes, rice and pastas for variety.

Eat more millet, buckwheat and brown rice – especially millet
Eat more 'live' natural yoghurts
Eat home-made chicken broth (every day if unwell)
Eat more onions, leeks, garlic, carrot, tomatoes, and broccoli
Eat more herbs–mint, thyme, and rosemary and especially parsley.

Kitchen Tools and Equipment Needed
- Large Casserole Pot for cooking chicken stock in the oven or, a large Pressure Cooker to take a chicken or bones on the hob.
- Juice Extractor – for extracting juices from fruits and vegetables
- Saucepans should only be cast iron enamelled, steel or stainless steel.
- Sealed glass jars for grains, pulses.
- Small Liquidiser or Coffee Grinder for grinding flax seeds
- Glass or Plastic containers for storing stock (not metal).

Why We Cook With These Oils
The oils and fats used are by and large one of the most important aspects to cooking safely, and I really mean safety for our body. Like many others before me and up to my illness I was unaware of some of the hazards to cooking with the wrong oils and fats. To help you I have shown what is good and what is bad – and why.

As I explained in earlier chapters fats and oils are divide into basically three groups: saturated, monounsaturated and polyunsaturated.

Sources Of Saturated Fat:
Short chained fatty acid
Butyric Acid from Butter - *Soluble at body temperature*
Although soluble in the blood at body temperature, when you consume too much butter the body has to turn it into a long chain fatty acid so that it can be stored and called on later when energy is required. Butter is good for the intestinal tract but keep the amount you consume to sensible proportions. Use butter in place of soft margarines for pastry. Use a small knob of butter when using olive oil, it will add a little flavour.

Medium chained fatty acids
Coconut Oil. Cocoa Oil, Palm Oil, Palm Kernel Oil *Solid at body temperature*
When we consumed too much short chain and medium chain fatty acids than our body needs or requires for energy, they are converted into long chain fatty acids and stored in the body for later use. Once they have been converted to the long chain fatty acid, the body can only use them for energy. They then must be burnt up providing us with calories. Coconut oil is excellent to cook with especially if you add a small knob of butter to give some extra flavour. Personally Cocoa, Palm and Palm Kernel oils are not favourites of mine.

Long chained fatty acids
Beef, Chicken Skin, Ham, Lamb, Lard, Pork and Suet. -*Solid at body temperature*
Processed and commercially produced pastries, breads and baked goods, contents of pies and non-dairy cream substitutes and most processed and fast food produce use this type of long chain

saturated fatty acids. Do not use any of these in any form of cooking if you are unwell. Consume in moderation if you are fit and well.

Sources of Monounsaturated Fat: Olive Oil. This is my favourite and with a small knob of butter added gives a clean taste and flavour to cooked foods. Only use Extra Virgin Olive Oil and find one which your palate prefers as they differ dependant upon the region and source. Always keep olive oil in a dark cupboard, but not in a refrigerator.

Sources of Polyunsaturated Fat: Flaxseed and Borage seed Oils
Do Not Cook With Flaxseed Oil
Under the strict cooking regime of the oil/protein programme none of these should be used for cooking. Corn oil, Sunflower, Safflower, Sesame seed, Pumpkin seed, Peanut, Walnut, Almonds, Pecan.

Is Organic Best?
Vegetable and Fruit: Organic foods are grown as close to natural methods as possible. But, organic farming still uses some herbicides approved by the Soil Association™. The major downside in purchasing organic food is the extra cost, in some

cases as much as 50% more expensive in fresh fruit and vegetable and as much as twice the cost for organic meat. Having indicated these additional costs, I still believe there is an important case for eating organic produce, but there is still something of a lottery with imported organic produce as to whether or not it meets the high standards that we expect of it. If your budget runs to be able to afford buying organic then there may be a health advantage, particularly for anyone who is unwell. If you think it is not worth the additional cost, then if you follow good hygiene and cleansing you will have excellent healthy food.

Meat is a slightly different matter, for those who are chronically ill they need all the advantages from fresh clean food. My choice is always fresh wild meat first and then fresh organically reared meat as an alternative; but both in moderation as the body finds it much more stressful in digesting meat than vegetables and fruits.
When the Almighty was a young omni-presence he looked down on man and woman and he saw how they gathered their nuts and hay, because that is what the homo sapien was doing in those dim and distant days. The important point is that the grains and the food that man ate were high in essential nutrients and oils.

Is meat healthy?
We have to understand that there is three types of meat available to us and they're availability appear in order.
- Commercial intensively reared meats
- Organically reared meat
- Wild meat

The healthiest meat we can consume is 'wild' meat which man has had no hand in artificially feeding, inoculation with hormones or dousing with organo-phosphates.
Wild meat has a lower level of tissue fat and very often 10 fold lower than intensively reared animals. Domesticated cattle, commercially reared can contain as much as 30% fat content within the animals meat tissue. It is not just the amount of fat in the tissue that is important, it is the ratio of both saturated and

unsaturated fats found within the tissue that is important. An article in *Positive Health* magazine by Lisa Saffron reported that the ratio of unsaturated to saturated fats in intensively reared animals is 1:50, whereas in wild animals it is 1:2.3. Also, wild cattle meat contains more than three times as much protein as fat than intensively reared animals.

If these fat ratios are an important indicator, as they are; then the ratio in wild animals is much closer to what we require as an intake of both saturated and unsaturated fat to stay healthy.

Yes - we do need saturated fats in our diet.

If, as what is presently being argued by the scientists, that red meat is a possible link to chronic illness and even cancer then the lower the fat content of the meat tissue we consume the better it is for us. It makes little difference if you trim the fat from domesticated, intensely reared produced meat, the high fat content is still contained in the flesh tissue. Recent research (June 2001) however, questions whether red meat is linked to cancer.

Between the 'wild' cattle and the intensively reared cattle, organically reared cattle are playing 'piggy in the middle' (excuse the pun again) at the moment. Their fat content does not fall quite as low as wild meat nor is the ratio of saturated and unsaturated quite as good as 'wild' animal meat, but organic meat has a better fat profile and tissue content than intensively farmed animals.

Lisa Saffron also mentions in her article that the World Cancer Research Fund (WCRF) have recently published an extensive, monumental review of linking some foods and nutrition to cancer. The WCRF have concluded that eating a high proportion of red meat may lead to a possible greater risk of some cancers namely prostate, pancreatic cancer, colorectal cancer, breast and kidney cancer.

What the WCRF have not evaluated or considered is to compare the risk factors (if there are any) in red meat in relation to the three different types of meats available to us.

What the WCRF have done is given us data and research based upon the consumption of intensively reared cattle meat - there is no consideration or data in respect to organic or wild cattle meat.

They have classed all red meats the same irrespective of how they have been reared. All red meats have been tarred with the same brush so to speak.
The innocent condemned with the guilty.

Conclusion:
The research on 'red meat' was conducted with commercial intensively reared cattle, where the fat profile is not good and the meat tissue fat content is high. If the research had included wild and organic meats, it may well have shed a completely different light on the red meat/cancer argument and come to a different conclusion. There is now mounting evidence that saturated fats do not play such an important role in respect to some degenerative diseases.
WCRF-Recommendations:
As a result of their research the World Cancer Research Fund have recommended a reduction in our consumption of red meat to 80g (3 ounces) of red meat per day, with additional advice to consumers to eat fish, poultry or meat from wild stock in preference.

Identifying good flaxseed oil is not so easy. Although some oil processors go along the 'organic' route, in particular with flaxseed some crop years due to the inclement weather the organic crop can fall below the required standard. Food grade flaxseed for processing oil is best from a Grade 1 selected seed source and especially the Brown flaxseed from Canada.
How to buy – look for: Pesticide and Additive Free, Cold Pressed, Oxygen Free and UV and Heat Protected.

Preparing Vegetables:
Peel or trim vegetables as economically as possible, this retains much of the nutritional goodness of the vegetable.
Never use badly bruised or mould ridden vegetable. Wash and rinse vegetables thoroughly.

Wherever possible vegetables should be soaked in salt water for 5 - 10 minutes, drained, rinsed and then cooked. This soaking enables the removal of small insects or slugs. You should pay particular attention to leek and spinach, making sure they are clean.

Root vegetables should be scrubbed with a nail brush, especially if they are to be cooked with the skin on. Many vegetables can be cooked with their skin on, this is a more nutritious way of eating vegetables – but, make sure they are clean before cooking. When preparing potatoes immerse them in cold water immediately after peeling.

Cooking Vegetables
Always use steel, stainless steel or cast iron.
Do not use aluminium pans.

Vitamins A, B and particularly Vitamin C are found in most vegetables as well as a host of beneficial enzymes. Vitamin C is, however, an unstable vitamin and much of it can be lost with incorrect storage and preparation. Also prolonged soaking or cooking, the addition of bi-carbonate of soda, destroys vitamin C. Bicarbonate of soda used to be used to maintain the colour of green vegetable during cooking, but this loss of colour was always due to overcooking. When cooking vegetables use only sea salt when called for and never refined cooking salt.

Braising vegetables is an excellent way of cooking and presenting a dish. Braising also tends to retain more of the nutrients in vegetables, plus by using home made stocks for the braising stock/liquid such as our chicken stock mentioned, the nutritional value is tremendous, especially for the unwell or convalescing.

What Oil Is Best For Cooking
Many nutritional experts now agree that the best oils for cooking are coconut oil, olive oil and butter. These oils are composed

chiefly of oleic acid, a monounsaturated oil that is more resistant to the damaging effects of heat compared to highly polyunsaturated oils like corn, safflower and soy. When polyunsaturated oils are exposed to heat, the chemical structure of the essential fatty acids is changed to toxic derivatives known as lipid peroxides.

DO NOT COOK DIRECTLY WITH FLAXSEED OIL.

The Super Health Foods

There are some foods that are packed full of nutritionally valuable compounds, vitamins and minerals. These foods can be considered 'super foods' for our body's well being. Many of these foods are ideally balanced nutritionally in that they can be assimilated within the body very easily. Make every effort to include them within your diet somehow.

Almonds: an important source of the minerals iron, magnesium, potassium and zinc. Eat vitamin C rich food at the same time, as almonds contain oxalic acid and phytic acid, which can prevent the absorption of this vitamin.

Apricots: Choose the fruit that has the best full colour. The brighter the fruit the higher levels of beta-carotene they contain. Also high in vitamin A.

Avocado: the fruit that is almost a complete food. Rich in potassium and vitamin A.

Barley: has a very high mineral content with calcium, potassium and vitamin B-complex. Ideal for combating stress or fatigue. Add a handful of barley to casserole or stew. Good for lowering blood cholesterol levels in the body.

Beetroot: has been used for many hundreds for years for anaemia and liver problems. Aids the digestive system especially when grated raw with apple and carrot topped with the juice of a lemon and olive oil.

Broccoli: A member of the crucifer family, which consists of Brussel sprouts, cabbage, cauliflower – broccoli has a protective effect against infections and disease. Rich in, beta-carotene, folic acid, iron and vitamin C.

Carrots: Rich in vitamin A, a single raw carrot chewed on every day will supply all your days Vitamin A requirements.

Celery: Celery is high in calcium, aids in removing waste via the urine due to a positive effect on the kidneys. Hypocrites said celery calms the nerves.

Cider Vinegar: has a very high mineral content due to the fermentation from whole fresh apple juice to prepare this vinegar.

High in calcium, potassium, phosphorus, sodium and trace elements. It increases blood oxygenation, improves metabolism, strengthens digestion and increases blood clotting ability. **Two teaspoons a day in water first thing in the morning is useful for individuals with weight problems. Additional information at the end of this section.

Garlic: Garlic has a high reputation and justifiably so in fighting infections. Some stories and myths abound but more recently with a serious epidemic of influenza in the city, the Russians flew in 500 ton of garlic in to help combat the disease, it worked. Garlic has been proved to be a great antiseptic both internally and externally. Garlic will also aid in clearing fat deposits from the blood, lowers cholesterol and protects against viral and bacterial infections.

Grapes: Grape fasting, by eating nothing except grapes for two days with clean water has excellent cleansing, detoxifying and regenerating effects on the body. An ideal food for those convalescing, but also for anyone suffering with depression or fatigue. Purple grape juice found to increase Nitric Oxide by 70%, improved dilation of the blood vessels and blood flow to extremities.

Kelp: A superb source of many mineral and vitamins including iodine which helps to protect the body from atmospheric radiation as well as aging too early. Rich in B-complex vitamins, vitamins D, E and K, magnesium and calcium. Improves hair and nails. You will need to take 6 to 8 tablets/capsules following each meal for beneficial results.

Lecithin: Working at the cellular level, lecithin helps to prevent stress and is important for maintaining a healthy nervous system. A daily supplementation allows the body fats to be converted into energy much more quickly, and existing fats deposits will slowly disperse. Lecithin breaks down cholesterol so that it can pass through the artery walls, and has been shown to increase immunity to virus infections and aid in preventing gallstones. It has a cleansing activity on the liver and purifies the kidneys and, because of its chlorine and unsaturated fatty acid contents it is very good for conditioning of the skin. Bought in granular form from health shops.

Molasses: The calcium content of black-strap molasses is as much as a glass full of milk, the iron content as nine eggs and more potassium than any other food. With an excellent vitamin B-complex balance. Molasses is what is left behind after the white refined sugar is taken from the sugar cane. It is rich in magnesium, vitamin E and copper and a worth while supplement for women with anaemia. Another benefit of molasses is that it will aid in the pH balance of the body. Take a tablespoon each day with the juice of half fresh lemon in a glass of warm/hot water at the start of the day. Not for diabetics.

Oats: have excellent soothing condition for the nerves, they are very high in calcium, magnesium, potassium together with vitamin B-complex. Oats aid in reducing cholesterol.
An excellent breakfast for children is oats cooked as porridge with a teaspoon each of honey and molasses and a tablespoon of flaxseed oil, especially on the morning of an exam.

Rabbit: Try to buy wild rabbit if possible. Normal reared rabbit has a much lower tissue fat profile than beef, lamb or pork and wild is even better plus the addition of important minerals and nutrients in the meat. Ideally cook slowly in an oven to retain the goodness and flavour.
An excellent casserole is to include prunes, Guinness ale, carrot, onion and pearl barley for a meal that is absolutely bursting with nutrition.

Sprouted Grains: As with flaxseed, sprouted grains have been used in the diet of man for thousands of years, especially the

Chinese. Sprouted grains are bursting with nutrition and really must be included in the diet at least two or three times a week. They are a live food nourishment rich in vitamins A, C, D, E, K and B-complex, calcium, potassium, phosphorus, magnesium, iron, high quality proteins and valuable plant enzymes. Sprouts are consumed at the peak of their nutritional value – 'when they are still growing'.

Spirulina: A single cell blue-green alga it is microscopic in size. As with all alga it thrives in water and in particular Lake Texoco in Mexico. Excellent for the treatment of anaemia and liver disorders. Useful in weight control, its proteins contain a high proportion of the amino acid phenlalanine, which is metabolised in to brain neurotransmitter substances, which control energy levels, appetite, mood and behaviour. Dose is generally three tablets 30 minutes prior to a meal. Spirulina has the effect of curbing appetite but maintaining a feeling of well-being.

Apple Cider Vinegar –Don't leave this out of your diet
Apple Cider Vinegar has been around as long as flaxseed. Seven thousand years ago the Babylonians would ferment the date from palms and created a date vinegar. At the time of Christ the Romans created different vinegars from such fruits as figs, grapes, and rye, depending on what part of the world they were conquering at the time. One of the important assets in Julius Caesar's army was their ability to stay fit and healthy – the legions would drink vinegar mixed with water for its nutritional healing and antiseptic properties. Hypocrites prescribed vinegar for his those patients that were unwell. Many other cultures have used vinegar through the ages and valued it for both its nutritional and its medicinal benefits. For centuries it was used to disinfect wounds as well as insect bites and snakebites.

What Nutrition is in ACV?
A host of vitamins, minerals, nutrients and substances are contained in ACV to aid health. The vitamins consist of beta-

carotene (a precursor to vitamin A), bioflavonoids, vitamin B1, B2, and B6, C and E. ACV has a multitude of enzymes and minerals, such as calcium, chlorine, iron, magnesium, phosphorus, potassium, sulphur, and many other trace elements. The cell wall of the fresh apples used for making cider vinegar contain tannins as well as acetic acid, malic acid, propionic acid, tartaric acid, and pectin.

What To Buy?
To get the best health advantages from ACV be sure to purchase organic, naturally fermented, unfiltered, unpasteurised. If You will know when you have the correct vinegar when you find a sediment at the bottom of the bottle.
Do NOT purchase white or distilled vinegar, it has none of the beneficial elements listed above.

Other benefits of ACV...
ACV has been credited with the ability in preventing the growth of bad bacteria and mould. By adding it to your diet as a nutritional supplement you will find additional health benefits.

Most conventionally grown fruit and vegetable have pesticide residues on the skin and bacteria from the soil. To remove this spray the produce with apple cider vinegar, leaving for 5 minutes and then rinse with water.

Apple Cider Vinegar has been known for centuries to ameliorate certain symptoms of illness and disease. The vinegar boosts the health of the ailing individual with its nutritional qualities.
ACV has been used as an effective remedy for arthritis, gout and kidney disease as well as alleviating some forms of joint pain. Just as flaxseed oil can aid calcium deposits, the malic acid in the apples dissolves calcium deposits that congregate in the wrong parts of the body. ACV has the unique ability to balance the acid-alkaline pH levels in the body and further aids in oxygenating the blood.

As a digestive aid ACV helps in breaking down minerals, protein and fats as well as inhibiting the growth of unfriendly bacteria in the digestive tract. ACV's detoxifying properties strengthen the immune system and may prevent bacterial, fungal and viral infections.

It has a natural anti-biotic effect and can be used for antibacterial and anti-inflammatory medicinal use.

The benefits also include reducing pulmonary and respiratory infections, and may help to reduce watery eyes and nasal discharge. As a preventative treatment against parasitic infection, both internal and external.

For many centuries people who have drunk apple cider vinegar have frequently felt better. Now scientists understand why! Apple Cider Vinegar contains cholesterol-reducing pectin and the perfect balance of 19 minerals, including potassium, phosphorus, chlorine, sodium, magnesium, calcium, sulphur, iron, fluorine and silicon. In fact, apple cider vinegar contains almost 100 different components that can help the body.

Some of the benefits from Apple Cider Vinegar: Many of the benefits of ACV are significantly enhanced when taken as part of your diet with flax seed oil.

- Promotes Digestion
- Assists in regulate blood pressure
- Improves Metabolism
- Helps flush out the Gall Bladder and Liver
- Assists Kidney in removal of toxins and fluids
- Assists in relieving Arthritic pain
- Helps fight infection

- Helps fight Osteoporosis
- Aids in Weight control with Flax seed oil
- Maintain healthy skin
- Relieves sore throats, laryngitis
- Soothes sunburn, shingles and bites
- Helps prevent dandruff, baldness and itching scalp

How Much to Take:

It is recommended that 1-tablespoon be taken in a small glass of water (100ml) before each meal. This method aids the digestive tract, helps to reduce bacteria infection from food and increases the digestive juices for processing food.

For those in a hurry throughout life and may not get a chance to take ACV at regular times I would recommend 1 tablespoon in water in the morning and if you get a chance take another portion later in the day (after noon).

See sources section to purchase 'Honeygar' Apple Cider Vinegar.

Recipes – Grand Ma Knew Best

Cooking with Flax
When you add flax seed to your cooking, you add a pleasant, nutty taste, and more. The attractive, oval reddish-brown seeds of flax add taste, extra texture and good nutrition to your breads and

other baked goods. That's why flax has been long-used in multi-grain cereals and snack foods. Flax seed also delivers the benefits of its soluble fibre, lignans, omega-3 fatty acid mix and protein.

Flax seed can be added to your cooking in its ground or whole seed form.

• **Whole flax seed -** The small, reddish-brown seeds of flax add tremendous nutritional value when added to bread dough, pancake, cake or biscuit mixes. When sprinkled on top of any of these before baking, they also add crunch, taste and eye appeal.

• **Ground flax seed** - Grind the flax seed to a free-flowing granular consistency in a coffee bean grinder or blender.

Flax seed replaces oils

Flax seed can stand in for all of the oil or fats called for in a recipe because of its high oil content. If a recipe calls for 100ml of oil, use 300gr of whole flax seed and then mill flax to replace the oil — a ratio of 3:1 substitution. Baked items tend to brown more rapidly with flax seed in the recipe instead of oil.

Storage

Whole flax seed that is dry and clean, can be stored at room temperature for up to a year. For optimum freshness, ground flax seed should be ground as needed, or refrigerated in an airtight, opaque container.

Flax seed Breads & Pastries

Orange Bran Flax Muffins
Whole oranges give these muffins a wonderful flavour.
Ingredients serves 18 muffins
375g Oat Bran
250g All purpose flour
250g Flaxseed
250g Natural Bran
15g Baking Powder
2g _ teaspoon salt
2 Whole Oranges - quartered and seeded

250g Natural Unrefined Brown Sugar
250ml Butter Milk
125ml Extra Virgin Olive Oil
2 Medium Eggs
_ teaspoon Baking Soda
375g sultanas and raisins

In a large bowl, combine oat bran, flour, flax seed, bran, baking powder and salt. Set aside.
In a blender or food processor, combine oranges, brown sugar, buttermilk, oil, eggs and baking soda. Blend well.
Pour orange mixture into dry ingredients. Mix until well blended. Stir in raisins.
Fill paper lined muffin tins almost to the top.
Bake in 190 C (375 • F) oven for 18 to 20 minutes or until wooden pick inserted in centre of muffin comes out clean.
Cool in tins 5 minutes before removing to cooling rack.
*Flax seed may also be ground. Measure first, then grind or mill.
**For chocolate lovers, substitute white chocolate chips for raisins.

Flax Fried Rice
Excellent as a light meal or a side dish... and kids love it!

Serves 6 with one cup each

250g long grain rice - 500ml water
_ teaspoon of sea salt
25ml/1 _ tablespoons of Extra Virgin Olive Oil
Medium eggs beaten
125 gr cooked chicken breast
Onion peeled and chopped
1 carrot slice thin length ways

12 - Cashews nuts
Tbsp Light Soy sauce
1 teaspoon of sesame oil
50g Flaxseed ** - toasted

Rinse rice well in a sieve under cold running water. In a medium saucepan, bring water and salt to a boil, add rice, bring to a boil again, stirring with a fork. Reduce heat, cover, simmer slowly 20 minutes. Remove lid, allow steam to escape. Fluff rice with a fork. Cool, cover and place in refrigerator overnight.
In a large non-stick skillet, over low/medium heat, heat olive oil. Add egg and fry until half cooked.
Add rice, breaking up any lumps, stirring quickly to coat the rice. Reduce heat to medium low; add chicken, vegetables and onions. Cook, turning rice mixture gently but frequently, about 4 minutes. Add soy sauce, sesame oil and flax seed. Reduce heat to low, cover and cook 3 minutes.
**To toast flax seed, spread flax seeds in small metal pan. Bake at 180°C (350°F) for 3 to 5 minutes. Stir while toasting.

Two-hour Buns
Simple and delicious... nothing beats fresh buns!

25g fast rising instant yeast (4x7g packs)
8 cups of Self raising flour
175g fresh ground flaxseed
125g granulated sugar
2 medium eggs

1 teaspoon of sea salt
750ml of tepid/warm water (250ml hot/500ml cold)

Makes 48 buns

In a bowl, mix yeast, 4 cups flour and ground flax.
In a large bowl, beat sugar, eggs and salt. Add water and stir.
Add flour mixture to the liquid and beat until well blended.
Add remaining flour and knead.
Put in a warm place for 15 mins to rise
Knead out the air and let rise again 15 minutes.
Knead again and form into buns.
Place on greased baking sheet allowing 5 cm/2 inches between buns. Allow to rise again in a warm place for one hour.
Preheat oven to 180°C (350°F).
Bake 20 minutes. Remove and cool on a rack.

Vegetarian Dishes

I am not forgetting the vegetarians who may be interested in the contents of this book. Many of the vegetable dishes can be converted to vegetarian dishes by simple replacing the chicken stock for vegetable stock. Vegetable stock recipe appears in the stock making section.

Vegetable Dishes

Glazed Carrots

It was not until Elizabeth I that carrots became a popular British dish. Over the centuries, when sugar has been scarce, carrots have been used to replace it in puddings, pies or preserves. In this recipe we have used honey to give an appetising glaze. Serve this vegetable with roast or game.

Preparation Time: 10 minutes
Cooking time: 20 – 30 minutes
Ingredients for 4
700g - Carrots, peeled; sliced into 2.5cm rounds
450ml - Chicken Stock
2 Tbsp (30ml) - Local Honey
75g - Butter, cut into small pieces
Some Freshly Ground Black Pepper
Pinch of Sea Salt
2 Tbsp - Fresh Chopped Parsley.

Prepare carrots and place in a saucepan with the stock, honey and butter. Season with pepper. Cover the pan and bring to the boil, lower heat and continue to simmer for around 20 minutes or until the carrots are tender and the liquid has reduced to a glaze. If the during the cooking the liquid is not reducing quick enough. Remove the lid from saucepan increase the heat to allow more evaporation towards the end of the cooking time.
Place warmed carrots in a warmed serving dish.
Sprinkle with salt and parsley to taste.

Vegetable Casserole
Preparation Time: 20 minutes
Cooking Time: 45 minutes
Pre-Heated oven 180•C (350•F) Gas Mk 4
Ingredients for 4
2 Large Potatoes, peeled and diced or sliced
_ Small Cauliflower, washed and broken into florets
_ cup Petit Pois
1 Large White Onion, peeled and sliced
1 Medium Courgette, washed and sliced
1 Red Pepper, deseeded and sliced
_ Celery Heart, washed and sliced
A handful of Watercress washed and roughly chopped
1 Large Leek, washed trimmed and sliced.

3 Medium Carrots, peeled and sliced along length
_ cup of Buckwheat Groats or Pearl Barley
5 Tablespoons of Olive Oil
25g Butter
Sea Salt and Fresh Ground Pepper
1 litre of Fresh made Chicken Stock
1 glass of Medium Sherry or White Wine
2 Tablespoons of Flour
_ teaspoon of Mixed Herbs or Herb de Provence
_ Bunch of Fresh Parsley

With a heavy based pan gently heat olive oil and butter. Add to the pan onion, leek, courgette and carrot for 5 minutes turning frequently. Add two tablespoons of flour mix well then add glass of Sherry or Wine, stir for 2 minutes.

To a large oven-proof casserole dish, add all of the vegetables, herbs and seasoning except the Parsley.

Fill to within 2.5cm of the top with the Chicken Stock. Cover and put in the pre-heated oven and cook for 40 minutes or until the vegetables are tender.

10 minutes before end of cooking add the Parsley. Serve hot with Butter Dumplings

Braised Leeks

The garden leek is one of six members of the onion family and has been around in Britain since pre-Norman times. The leek is the mildest of the family and has always been appreciated by the imaginative cook for its flavour and adaptability.

Preparation Time: 10 minutes
Cooking Time: 20 – 30 minutes
Pre-Heat Oven to 180(C (350(F)-Gas Mark 4
Ingredients For 4

8 - Leeks
300ml - Chicken Stock
50g - Butter, cut into pieces

Sea Salt
Freshly Ground Pepper
1 Tbsp - Chopped Parsley
Optional - Green Pepper Corns

Wash and Clean the Leeks thoroughly pulling apart the leaves to ensure no dirt or grit remains. Trim and Remove any damaged leaves. Trim the base and slice length ways along the white portion of the leek.

Grease an ovenproof dish with a small portion of the butter, then arrange the whole leeks in the dish.

Bring the stock to the boil in a separate saucepan. Pour the hot stock over the leeks and add season with the salt, pepper and add butter.

Cover the dish and bake in the pre-heated oven for 40 minutes. For a slightly glazed appearance remove the lid for the last 5 minutes of the cooking time.

Garnish with chopped parsley and peppercorns to suit taste.

The mild flavour of Leeks are particularly good with rich stews, but can also be used with most fish and meat dishes.

Braised Jerusalem Artichoke

French explorers in Canada introduced the Artichoke to Europe about 400 years ago. The artichoke can be cooked and served like potatoes; sautéed in butter, stewed whole in stock, mashed or sliced and baked au gratin. Artichokes can be served with a rich white sauce or braised gently as shown here.

Preparation Time: 15 minutes
Cooking Time: 45 minutes
Ingredients for 4

750g - Jerusalem Artichoke, peeled
25g - Butter
1 Tbsp - Olive Oil
1 - Onion, peeled and sliced thin
Clove Garlic, crushed (Optional)

1 – Tbsp Corn flour
1 – Cup of Medium White Wine
Sea Salt and Freshly ground Black Pepper
1 – Tbsp Chopped Parsley
1 – Tbsp Capers (Optional)

*In a heavy saucepan heat the butter and oil gently. Add the onions and garlic and gently fry for 5 or 6 minutes or until soft. Stir in the corn flour and cook gently over a low heat for 1 or 2 minutes, stirring frequently to prevent sticking and burning. Add white wine and bring to the boil stirring in the onion and garlic. Add the Artichokes and add water to just cover the Artichoke.
Season with salt and pepper.
Cover the saucepan with tight fitting lid and simmer for 45 minutes until cooked and tender.
Add more water during if water is evaporating too fast. Cooking time depends largely on the size of the Artichoke
Sprinkle with parsley and serve hot.*

Potato and Onion Bake

This is a superb dish that can be served on its own or accompany most meals roast meats, grilles or fish.

Preparation Time: 15 minutes
Cooking Time: 1 hour
Ingredients for Four
Pre Heated oven at 180•C (350•F) or Gas Mk 4

1 kg Maris Piper Potato or similar, peel and sliced thin
2 Large White Onions-peel and sliced thin
2 Tablespoons of Olive Oil
25g Butter
_ litre Fresh Chicken or Beef Stock
2 Teaspoons of Mixed Herbs or Herb de Provence
Sea Salt and Fresh Ground Black Pepper

Prepare two oven-proof dishes, lightly oiled with Olive Oil.
Put a layer of potato in the bottom of each dish. Season with a pinch of Sea Salt, Pepper and Mixed Herbs, repeat this seasoning on each layer.
Lay a tier of onion on the potato and season. Repeat this layering alternately with potato and onion until the vegetables are 12mm from the rim.
Finish with potato on top.
Pour the stock over the vegetable to _ of the way up to the vegetables.
Brush the final potato layer with butter and put in the oven for 45 to 50 minutes covered with foil. 10-15 minutes before the end remove the foil,
return to the oven and bake until top is browned.
Serve hot

Creamed Cabbage

Cabbage has often suffered disparagingly due to it frequently being over cooked and served with insufficient seasoning. This recipe changes all that, transforming its flavour and appearance.

Cabbage became popular in the 17th century when Sir Anthony Ashley brought the new variety to England from Holland.

Preparation time: 10 minutes
Cooking Time: 15 minutes
Ingredients for Four

500g - Cabbage, chopped coarsely
50g – butter
Clove of Garlic, finely chopped (optional)

_ tsp - Nutmeg, freshly ground
900ml - Double Cream
Sea Salt
Freshly Ground Black Pepper

Trim cabbage removing any damaged leaves. Wash, drain and dry thoroughly.
Melt the butter in a heavy frying pan and add the cabbage and the garlic.
Fry gently, stirring frequently to prevent sticking and burning for about 10 minutes or until the cabbage has softened but is still slightly crunchy.
Season with salt, nutmeg and pepper.
Stir in the cream and cook for a further 3 to 5 minutes – stir frequently.
When cooked serve immediately.
The perfect accompaniment with grilled and roast meats.

Stuffed Tomatoes

This versatile easy to prepare dish can be served as a first course, or an accompaniment to a main course or simply on it own. Tomatoes became popular around 250 years ago usually made into pickles with garlic, vinegar and ginger.

Preparation time: 10 minutes
Cooking Time: 20 minutes
Pre-Heat Oven to 180(C (350(F) Gas Mark 4
Ingredients for Four
4 – Large Tomatoes
1 – medium Onion, peeled and chopped
25g – Butter
100g – Mushroom washed, dried and chopped
2 Tbsp – Parmesan Cheese, grated
100g – Fresh Breadcrumbs

2 Tbsp – Fresh chopped Basil
Sea Salt and Freshly ground Black Pepper
_ tsp - Paprika

Wash the tomatoes and slice off the tops and reserve to one side.
Scoop out the centres with a spoon, make sure you do not break the skin and reserve the pulp into a mixing bowl, the skins keep separately to one side.
Melt butter in a frying pan over a low heat.
Add the onions and fry until soft and transparent.
Then add mushrooms and cook gently for a few minutes.
Put the mushroom and onion into the bowl with the pulp and add breadcrumbs, herbs and seasoning to taste.
Mix all the ingredients well.
Spoon the mixture into the centre of the topped tomatoes skins, sprinkle with cheese and paprika and replace the tomato tops.
Stand the tomatoes upright without
falling over into a ovenproof dish.
Place in pre-heated oven for 20 minutes, or until cooked.
Serve hot.

Mashed Celeriac And Potatoes

Celeriac has become much more popular in the past 10 years. Celeriac is a delicious vegetable, which can be braised in a chicken stock, sautéed, boiled, au gratin as a puree or in a green salad.

The recipe that follows goes particularly well with game or served alongside roast potatoes as an accompaniment to Rib of Beef.

Preparation Time: 15 minutes
Cooking Time: 20 minutes
Ingredients for Four
500g – Potatoes, peeled and cut even-sized pieces.
750g – Celeriac, peeled and cut into 1.5cm cubes.
50g – Butter
50ml – Double Cream

Sea Salt
Freshly Ground Black Pepper
Sprig of Parsley - Garnish

You'll need two saucepans to prepare this dish.
In one the Celeriac and the other the Potatoes.
Cover both vegetables with water and cook for about 20 minutes or until both are tender.
Drain vegetables.
In a liquidiser puree the Celeriac.
Mash the potatoes and add to the pureed Celeriac together with the butter and cream.
Mash both vegetables together and serve with a sprig of parsley.
Season with salt and pepper.

Cauliflower With Anchovy Sauce or Cheese Sauce

This is a delicious nutritious accompaniment for roasted meats, grilled meats or game. The milk used as a cooking liquid retains the whiteness of the cauliflower

Preparation Time: 10 minutes
Cooking Time: 35 – 40 minutes
Ingredients for 4

1 - Large Cauliflower / 1 pint - Milk
50g – tin of Anchovies, in brine water only, pounded in a mortar and pestle or liquidise in a blender
25g – Butter
2 Tbsp – Plain Flour
1 tsp – Tomato Puree

Freshly Ground Black Pepper / 1 Tbsp – Capers (optional)
The Anchovies may be substituted with either 50g grated Cheddar Cheese or Gruyiere

Trim the bottom of the cauliflower and remove the outer leaves.
Slice a cross in the solid stem of the cauliflower.
Put the milk in to a saucepan and bring slowly to the bowl.
Add the cauliflower reduce to a simmer and cook for 20 minutes.
Turn the cauliflower upside down during
the last 5 minutes of cooking,
the cauliflower should still be slightly firm.
Remove to a serving dish and keep warm under a low grill.
In a separate saucepan melt the butter and add the flour and cook gently making sure not to brown.
Add the milk from the cauliflower to the saucepan add bring to the boil, stirring frequently until flour and milk has thickened.
To the sauce add the tomato puree and the anchovies
or the cheese.
Stir the mix well and add the seasoning.
Pour the sauce over the cauliflower and serve at once.

Braised Fennel

This dish is not as popular in Britain as it is in Italy, where it is known as 'finocchio'. Choose fresh, white heads and serve the dish with fish, chicken or grilled meats. A slight aniseed flavour it can be served in many ways. In Umbria it is served with stalks and leaves chopped with garlic and used as a stuffing for suckling pig. The Venetians use fennel with risotto; pasta and pecorino cheese is a favourite of Calabria.

Preparation Time: 5 minutes
Cooking Time 60 minutes
Ingredients for 4
2- Medium Sized Heads of Fennel -
trimmed and quartered
50g – Butter
200ml – Chicken Stock

1 Tbsp – Lemon Juice
2 Tbsp – Parmesan Cheese
Sea Salt
Freshly ground Black Pepper

In a heavy saucepan melt the butter adding the fennel and cook gently, stirring so that the fennel is coated with the butter.
Pour the stock and lemon juice over the fennel, seasoning with salt and pepper..
Cover the saucepan with a lid and simmer for about 30 minutes until the liquid has almost evaporated and fennel is tender.
If the liquid stock has not evaporated enough remove the lid and turn up the heat for the last 5 minutes of cooking time.
Remove the fennel to an oven proof serving dish and sprinkle the fennel with the Parmesan cheese.
Place under a hot grill for 5 minutes until slightly browned.

Ratatouille

Classic, Colourful and Richly flavoured, this French dish an authentic recipe of the South of France. Two very important rules when making Ratatouille is that you use only olive oil and never add water. This dish can be served hot or cold with fresh bread or as an accompaniment to roast, grilled meat or chicken.

Preparation Time: 40 minutes
Cooking Time: 60 minutes
Ingredients for Six
500g – Courgettes / 2 – Large Aubergines
225g – Onions peeled and quartered
3 – Green Peppers, de-seeded and sliced thick
2 – Cloves of Garlic, finely chopped or crushed
500g – Tomatoes, skinned and sliced
Sea Salt and Freshly Ground Black Pepper
2 Tbsp - Virgin Olive Oil
1 Tbsp – Crushed Coriander seeds

1 Tbsp each – Fresh Basil & Parsley chopped

Wash the Aubergines and Courgettes and dry. Put them into a colander and sprinkle liberally with salt. Leave for about 40 minutes so as to draw some of the excess moisture from the vegetables. Dry with paper kitchen towel.

Heat the oil in a large heavy frying pan and add the quartered Onion and Peppers and cook for 5 minutes or until the Onions are transparent. Add the Aubergines, Courgettes and Garlic. Cover the pan with a tight fitting lid and cook gently for 10 minutes. Add the Tomatoes and Coriander seeds, season with salt and pepper, cover again and cook gently for 45 minutes.

Check from time to time that vegetables are not sticking to the bottom of the pan. When cooked adjust seasoning and garnish with basil and parsley. Serve as desired, hot or cold.

Skinning Tomatoes: Boil up a saucepan of water. Put three or four tomatoes into the water for a minute or two.

Remove with a slotted spoon and peel off skin.

Homemade Chunky Vegetable Broth

If you have not already made your stock, hurry up you don't know what you're missing. Refer to stock section. The following recipe will take about 35 minutes to prepare and serve. The vegetable stocks are bursting with nutrition and are part of the staple diet for the unwell.

Ingredients for 2 servings

600ml Fresh Home Made Chicken Stock *(refer to stock recipe)*
_ Medium White onion – roughly chopped
1 Clove Garlic Chopped
1 Large Carrot-peel and cut into strips or sliced thin
1 Stick of Celery-sliced thin (include leaves if available)
_ Red Pepper cut into thin strips
A Hand full of Cauli and Broccoli florets (frozen if necessary)
_ teaspoon of mixed herbs or Herb de Provence
1 Heaped Tbsp each of Buckwheat Groats and Millet flake

Sea Salt and Black Ground Pepper to taste.

Using a sauce pan add stock and bring to the boil adding buckwheat and millet to the stock stirring occasionally to prevent sticking.
Prepare vegetables and add to the stock, adjust seasoning with salt and pepper.
Cook until vegetables are tender

Combinations of vegetables can be altered to suit own taste

Meat Dishes
Poultry, Game and Wild Meats
COOKING POULTRY
Poussin: A 4-8 week old chicken weighing up to 575g. It can be roasted, spit roast or grilled. When roasting place a knob of butter inside the cavity. If spit roasting baste with oil frequently.
Spring Chicken: Between 12-14 weeks old and 900g-1kg. It can be roasted, spit roasted or grilled.
Roasting Chicken or Broiler: This is a 4 month to 9 month bird. Weighing 1.4kg to 1.8kg
Capon: A neutered cockerel specially bred for its good meat. Excellent for roasting. Most capons weight 2.3kg to 3.6kg
Turkey: A medium size turkey is best weighing around 5kg. The best are hen birds 6-8 weeks old. When cooking turkey make sure it is bard well and basted during cooking as the meat can end up dry.

Duck: Most duck are between 1.8kg and 2.7kg. There is less meat in proportion to weight than on a chicken. Duck is a fatty meat so always prick the skin before cooking.

NEVER serve poultry undercooked. To check if the bird is ready for serving, insert a skewer into the thickest part of the thigh. If the juice run clear when you remove the skewer then the bird is ready. If, however, the juice are pinkish then the bird will need cooking longer.

Guide To Roasting Times Roasting Temperatures-180(C (350(F) Gas Mk 4

Type	Weight	Time in Minutes	
Chicken	450g-3.6kg	15-20 min/450g	+ 20 minutes
Duck	1.4kg-2.7kg	20 mins	/450g + 30 minutes
Turkey	2.7kg-4.5kg	20 mins	/450g + 20 minutes
Turkey	4.5kg-8.1kg	15 mins	/450g + 15 minutes
Goose	2.7kg-4.5kg	20 mins	/450g + 30 minutes

Golden Fried Wild Rabbit

This is a very popular dish in Italy using wild rabbit, and there are many different variations, but this is one of my favourites from a time spent in Porto Fino.

Preparation time: 20 minutes
Marinating time 60 minutes
Cooking Time 10 minutes
Ingredients for 4
1 Wild Rabbit, prepared by the butcher -
125g – Dry, White Breadcrumbs
50g – Butter / 50g - Plain Flour
1 tsp – Sea Salt
2 – Medium Eggs, beaten
75ml – Virgin Olive Oil
Marinade:
The Juice of a Lemon
2 Tbsp Virgin Olive Oil

1 – Small Onion, peeled and finely chopped
Sea Salt and Fresh Ground Black Pepper

Cut rabbit into small serving pieces. Place them in a bowl. Make the marinade by combining all the ingredients. Season well with salt and pepper and pour this over the rabbit.
Allow meat to marinade for no less than 60 minutes, turning often to get good distribution over the meat.
Mix the flour and salt and spread over a clean plate. Spread the breadcrumbs over another plate. Place the beaten eggs in a bowl. Dip each piece of meat first in the flour, then into the beaten egg and then roll in the breadcrumbs, covering evenly. Heat oil and butter together in a heavy frying pan. Fry the pieces of rabbit for about 8-10 minutes over a gentle heat, turning once or twice to get an even golden colour to the crust. Drain on kitchen paper and garnish with parsley and lemon wedges. Serve the Golden Fried Rabbit with a green salad, a side dish of spaghetti or dressed with a savoury butter.

Roast Stuffed Chicken
Preparation Time: 30 minutes
Cooking Time: Approximately 90 minutes
Pre-Heat Oven 200(C (400(F) Gas Mk 6
Ingredients for 4 to 6
1 – Large (1.8kg) Roasting Chicken/Small Capon
25g - Butter
For the Stuffing:
4–slices 2 day old bread, remove crusts & crumb
150ml – Milk / Chicken liver
_ Tbsp – Dried Mixed Herbs
Grated Rind and Juice of 1 Lemon
1 – Small Onion, chopped finely
40g – Butter / 1 Tbsp – Ground Almonds
Sea Salt and Fresh Ground Black Pepper

Remove giblets and set liver to one side. Rinse chicken in cold water and dry off. For stuffing: Liquidise bread in a blender add a little milk so that they are moist and leave for 20 minutes to absorb the milk. Add the chopped liver, herbs, lemon rind and juice, onion, butter and almonds. Mix well season with salt and pepper. Spoon the stuffing mix into the neck cavity until the breast is plump, but not too tight. Secure with skewer. Use remainder to stuff the bird from the tail end or shape them into forcemeat balls. Grease a roasting tin lightly. Rub butter into breasts and legs, and lightly sprinkle with salt and pepper. Cover loosely with greaseproof paper. Roast in centre of pre-heated oven for 1 hour. Reduce oven temperature to 180C, remove greaseproof paper, baste well and cook for a further 30 minutes –
Set aside and keep warm.

For Gravy: 300ml – Fresh homemade Chicken Stock
To make gravy, add the chicken stock to the roasting pan, scrape the pan whilst bringing to the boil on a hob. If you wish to thicken remove 3 Tbsp of stock, mix in 2 Tbsp of Corn Flour and add to the pan and meat juices, stir often.

Italian Chicken Breast

Ingredients for 2
2 free range skinless chicken breasts
large knob of butter
a slug of extra virgin oil
fresh tarragon or dried
1 lemon

Method
Place the breasts skin side down on a cutting board and pull away the two segments shaped like little torpedoes. Turn them over and using a sharp flat bladed knife cut lengthways through the breast leaving you with six thin pieces of chicken.

Heat a large knob of butter and a 3 tablespoons of olive oil in frying pan and when foaming drop in the chicken pieces – cook for 2 minutes maximum.

Before 2 minutes are up, add a handful of torn tarragon or a shake of dried, a good squeeze of lemon juice and rattle the pan about a bit and serve

Italian Chicken Kiev with Quick Tomato Sauce

Preparation Time 10 to 30 mins
Cooking Time 10 to 30 mins
Ingredients for 4
4 x 100g/3_oz chicken breasts, boneless and skinless
75g/3oz mozzarella, grated / 75g/3oz ricotta
60ml/4tbsp parmesan, freshly grated
15ml/1tbsp capers, rinsed and chopped
2 sun-dried tomatoes in oil, drained and chopped
15ml/1tbsp fresh basil, shredded
5ml/1tsp sun-dried tomato purée
75g/3oz fresh white fine breadcrumbs
25g/1oz plain flour / 2 eggs, beaten
salt and freshly ground black pepper

Method
Taking a small knife, cut each chicken breast horizontally to make a pocket.
Place breasts between sheet of greaseproof paper and beat to flatten slightly.
Combine mozzarella, ricotta, half the parmesan, capers, sun-dried tomatoes and tomato purée. Season generously with pepper and spoon some of the mixture into each chicken pocket.
Push filling in so that it is completely enclosed.
Place breadcrumbs and remaining parmesan in a shallow dish, season and mix well. On separate plate add flour and season. In a shallow dish have beaten egg ready.
Dust chicken breasts with flour, dip in egg then breadcrumbs to cover completely. Chill until ready to cook.
Heat a deep fat fryer and cook coated chicken for 8-10 minutes until cooked through and golden. Drain and serve immediately with tomato sauce (see below) and green salad.

Italian Chicken Kiev continued….

Quick tomato sauce
30ml/2tbsp olive oil
1 small onion, chopped finely
4 rashers streaky bacon, chopped
2 cloves of garlic, crushed
15ml/1tbsp chopped fresh thyme leaves
400g/14oz tomato pasta sauce
pinch crushed chilli flakes
sea salt and freshly ground black pepper
Heat a pan and add olive oil. Add onion, bacon, garlic and thyme and cook for 2-3 minutes until soft but not coloured.

Add tomato sauce and chilli flakes and simmer for 4 minutes, stirring occasionally, until reduced and thick. Season to taste.

Italian Style Ricotta Chicken
Preparation Time 10 to 30 mins
Cooking Time 30 mins to 1 hr
Ingredients for 4
4 medium/large freerange chicken breasts
4 rashers of back bacon / 1 tub ricotta
8 sun-dried tomatoes, coarsely chopped
good handful of basil, coarsely chopped
30ml/2tbsp olive oil / salt and pepper
For the Tomato Sauce
15ml/1tbsp olive oil
1 red onion, peeled and finely chopped
3 rashers bacon, cubed / 6 mushrooms, sliced or quartered
400g/14oz tinned chopped tomatoes

4 sun-dried tomatoes, coarsely chopped
5g/1 tsp sugar / 1 tbsp fresh basil
salt and pepper

Method
*Mix the ricotta, sun-dried tomatoes and the basil together. Chill.
Lay each chicken piece in a freezer bag and beat with a rolling pin to flatten. When each is even, remove and season.
Spoon the ricotta mix into each piece, leaving a gap around the edges. Roll each breast up, then wrap the bacon around them, securing with cocktail sticks.
Heat the olive oil in a frying pan and seal each breast before placing in the oven for 30 - 40 minutes - 190C/375/Gas5.
For the tomato sauce, heat the olive oil in a small pan then add the onion. After the onion has started to soften add the bacon and mushrooms and cook for a further 2 minutes. Add the tomatoes, season and leave to simmer gently for 5 minutes. Finally, add the sun-dried tomatoes.
Once the chicken is cooked remove from the oven and serve on a bed of pasta with the tomato sauce, salad and the fresh basil*

Porto's Pasta & Salad Dish
Cooking Time: 10 to 30 mins / Ingredients for 4
340g/12oz Pasta
400g/14oz tin chopped tomatoes
sprinkling of fresh chopped basil
2 cloves garlic, peeled and finely chopped
15ml/1tbsp mixed Italian herbs
Pinch of mild chilli powder / 1 onion, peeled and chopped
pinch of salt and pepper / sprinkling of sugar

Salad
1 onion, peeled and chopped
8 baby tomatoes, chopped into quarters
1 small lettuce, roughly shredded / 1 cucumber, diced

1 small red cabbage, roughly shredded
1 red pepper + 1 green pepper, seeded and diced
1 yellow pepper +1 orange pepper, seeded and diced
30ml/2tbsp olive oil
salt and pepper / a pinch of Italian herbs
5-10ml/1-2tsp sugar / 10ml/2tsp red wine vinegar
55g/2oz grated cheese

Method
Firstly, cook the pasta according to the instructions on the packet. In a separate saucepan, on a moderate heat pour the tinned tomatoes and add the basil, garlic, Italian herbs, onion, salt, pepper, chilli powder and sugar. Stir these all together well and let simmer until thick, allowing all the flavours to develop.
Next, take the second onion, the baby tomatoes, lettuce, cucumber and peppers and toss it all into a clean bowl. Add the olive oil, vinegar, salt, pepper, herbs and sugar and toss it all together. Mix the cooked pasta in the saucepan with the tomato sauce and stir until the pasta is thoroughly covered with sauce.
Dish the pasta onto plates, sprinkle with a little grated cheese, and serve with the salad on the side.

Herbed Cauliflower and Pasta

Ingredients
125g/4oz Tricolore pasta
2 large leeks, trimmed and sliced into rounds
1 medium cauliflower, cut into florets
30ml/2tbsp olive oil
a pinch of basil /a pinch of oregano
a pinch of Italian seasoning / salt and black pepper
4 rashers middle cut bacon, trimmed and cut into 1cm/ 1/2in strips
125g/4oz mushrooms, sliced
2 large onions, peeled and sliced
125g/4oz Parmesan or mozzarella, grated
4 tomatoes, sliced, optional

Method
Place the pasta into a pan of boiling salted water and cook for about 2 minutes.
Add the leeks and cauliflower and cook for a further 8 minutes. Drain and set to one side. Pour oil into a frying pan and heat. Allow the basil, oregano, Italian seasoning, salt and pepper to cook for a few minutes and then add the bacon, mushrooms and onions. Cook until dark brown then remove the pan from the heat and set aside.
Place half of the bacon and mushroom mixture into a shallow heatproof serving dish, cover with all of the leek and cauliflower mix, and then top with the rest of the bacon and mushroom mixture. Sprinkle the cheese over the top and decorate with the tomato slices. Cook under a hot grill for about 5 minutes until the cheese has melted, and serve

Mediterranean Pasta
Preparation; 10 mins
Cooking time: 10 – 30 mins

Ingredients for 2
200g/7oz pasta
800g/1_lb tinned plum tomatoes, chopped
75ml/5tbsp olive oil
15ml/1tbsp chilli oil
5ml/1tsp salt / white pepper to taste
Italian herb mix
10ml/2tsp sugar
2 big cloves garlic, peeled and crushed

40g/1_oz capers in brine, drained / 80g/3oz black olives

Method

Cook the pasta in lightly salted boiling water.

Place the tomatoes into a separate heavy pan.

Add the olive oil, chilli oil, salt, pepper, herbs, sugar and garlic.
Boil on a high heat until the sauce thickens.

Adjust the seasoning and add the capers and olives.

Stir into the drained pasta and serve.

Chopped crispy streaky bacon may be added to the sauce for extra taste

Calabrian Minestra

Preparation and Cooking Time: 45 mins
Ingredients for 4

60ml/4tbsp extra virgin olive oil
1 red onion, peeled and finely chopped
2 medium carrots, peeled and cubed
3 medium potatoes, peeled and cubed
1 small Savoy cabbage, cored and sliced
1 hot Italian sausage, sliced
6 medium ripe tomatoes, skinned and chopped

Approx 500ml Chicken or vegetable stock
1 celery stalk, chopped
1 packet of macaroni

Method
Heat the olive oil in a pan and fry the onions with the sausage on a gentle heat for a couple of minutes
Add the cabbage, potatoes, carrots and celery and continue cooking until it is all soft
Add the tomatoes and the vegetable stock until covered by stock and simmer for 30 minutes. Add salt and pepper to taste
Boil the macaroni until it is half cooked, drain and add to the vegetables
Simmer until the pasta is cooked and serve with grated Parmesan cheese

Italian Chicken and Tomato Chutney
Preparation Time: Less than 10 mins
Cooking Time: 10 to 30 mins
Ingredients for 2

Italian Chicken: 2 Chicken Breasts
1 tsp dried Sage / Olive oil
2 slices of ham / 55g/2oz Camembert
55g/2oz Brie / 55g/2oz Stilton
Salt and pepper
Chutney: 1 red pepper, seeded and diced
1 medium onion, finely diced
1 chilli, chopped / 4 ripe tomatoes

2 tbs vinegar / 4 tbs brown sugar

Method
*Heat a griddle pan.
Beat and flatten the Chicken breasts and sprinkle with sage and season- brush or rub olive oil into both sides.
Mix cheeses together well, add seasoning.
Heat a heavy based pan, add a little olive oil and all the chutney ingredients and cook until soft. Season.
Put the chicken onto a hot griddle and cook on both sides.
Heat the grill. Place a good spoonful of the chutney onto chicken, and top with the cheese mixture. Add a slice of ham and place under hot grill, cook until the cheese starts to melt and the ham becomes slightly crispy.
To serve, drizzle a little olive oil over the top, and season well.
Serve with a salad of choice and some hot, crusty bread.*

Fish Dishes

Chicken and Prawn Creole
Cooking Time: 60 mins

Ingredients for 4
675g/1_lb boneless, skinless chicken
15ml/1tbsp vegetable oil
2 onions, coarsely chopped / 3 cloves garlic, chopped
1 each red and green pepper coarsely chopped
1 can (800g/28 oz) tomatoes
1 litre chicken stock
5ml/1tsp dried thyme / 5ml/1tsp dried oregano

1ml/_tsp cayenne pepper
450g/1lb long grain rice
450g/1lb medium prawns (fresh or frozen)
20g/_oz chopped fresh parsley

Method

In large non-stick pan, heat oil on medium heat and cook chicken until lightly browned. Add onions and garlic and cook for several minutes or until softened.
Add peppers and tomatoes, breaking up with back of spoon. Add stock, thyme, oregano and cayenne; bring to boil.
Stir in rice and cover, reduce heat and simmer for 20 minutes or until most of the liquid is absorbed.
In separate saucepan of boiling water, cook prawns for 3 minutes and drain. Peel and de-vein if necessary. Add prawns to rice mixture and cook for 5 minutes or until prawns are hot.
Stir in parsley and serve

Barbecued Trout with Fennel Butter

Preparation Time: Over 1 hr
Cooking Time: Less than 10 mins
Ingredients for 4

4 Whole trout
1 Tbsp chopped fresh thyme
2 Tbsp extra virgin olive oil
Sea Salt and Fresh Ground Pepper
Fennel Butter:
2 Tsp fennel seeds
125g Butter, softened

1 Tbsp chopped fresh parsley
2 Tsp Lemon juice

Method

*Wash and dry the trout inside and out, with a sharp knife make several cuts on each side. Mix together the thyme leaves, oil and some sea salt and pepper and rub over the fish making sure the flavourings
are pressed well into the cuts.
Marinate for at least 1 hour.
Make the butter. Toast the fennel seeds in a dry frying pan until they turn golden and release their aniseed aroma.
Cool and grind to a fine powder in a spice mill
or pestle and mortar.
Beat into the butter with the parsley, lemon juice and some pepper. Chill until required.
Brush the fish with a little extra oil and cook on a hot barbecue for 3-4 minutes each side until charred and cooked through. Rest for a few minutes and serve with the fennel butter and a tomato and olive salad.*

San Margarita Monkfish

Preparation Time 10 to 30 mins
Cooking Time 10 to 30 mins

Ingredients for 2

Olive oil for frying
1 large onion, peeled and roughly chopped
4 medium red potatoes, sliced
2 cups hot water
15ml/1tbsp tomato ketchup
15ml/1tbsp tomato puree

Sea Salt and Freshly Ground Black Pepper
15ml/1tbsp hot paprika
15ml/1tbsp sweet paprika
15ml/1tbsp saffron
2 monkfish fillets, trimmed and roughly chopped

Method

Heat the olive oil in a large saucepan and fry the onions slowly. When they are soft and beginning to caramelise, add the sliced potatoes as a single layer on top of the onions.
Fry for a few minutes together.
Place the water in a deep mixing bowl and add the tomato ketchup, puree, seasoning, paprika, sweet paprika and saffron. Combine and then pour mixture over the onions and potatoes.
Leave to simmer, covered for 15 minutes.
When the potatoes are half cooked (keep checking them during the 15 minutes) add the monkfish to the pan. Cook the fish for 5-6 minutes before turning and cooking the other side.
When the monkfish has finished cooking for another 5-6 minutes, take the pan off the heat and allow to stand for
5 minutes before serving.

Fisherman's Pie

Preparation Time: 10 mins
Cooking Time: 30 mins to 1 hr
Ingredients for 4
1 large potato, scrubbed and sliced thinly
225g/8oz Coley fillets, 225g/8oz cod fillets
2 sticks celery, trimmed and sliced
75g mushrooms, wiped and sliced
1 medium leek, trimmed and sliced
300ml/1/2 pint fish stock, or home-made stock
30ml/2tbsp corn flour / 200ml Skimmed milk
10ml/ 2tsp English mustard

50g frozen sweet corn / 30ml/2tbsp freshly chopped chives
2 medium tomatoes, sliced thinly
50g reduced fat cheddar cheese, grated

Method

Preheat oven to 200C/400F/Gas 6. Place the potato in a saucepan and cover with water. Bring to the boil and cook for 4-5 minutes until tender. Drain well and set aside. Wash the fish and place in a frying pan. Add the celery, mushrooms and leek. Pour over the stock, bring to the boil, cover and simmer for 5-6 minutes until the fish is tender. Drain fish and vegetables, reserving 85ml of the cooking liquid. Discard skin from the fish, and flake into bite-sized pieces. Set aside. Blend the corn flour with 60ml/4tbsp milk to form a paste. Pour remaining milk into a saucepan with the reserved cooking liquid. Stir in the corn flour paste. Bring to the boil, stirring until thickened. Remove from the heat and stir in the fish, vegetables, mustard, sweet corn and chives. Mix well and pile into the base of an oven proof pie dish. Arrange the sliced tomatoes on top, then the sliced potato. Sprinkle with cheese and bake in the oven for 20-25 minutes until golden.

Curried Prawns With Naan Bread

Preparation Time: 10 to 30 mins
Cooking Time: 10 to 30 mins
Ingredients for 4
22.5ml/1_tbsp vegetable oil
2 onions, peeled and sliced
1 clove garlic, peeled and crushed
450g/1lb tomatoes, peeled and roughly chopped
22.5ml/1_tbsp curry paste
15ml/1tbsp mango chutney
450g/1lb frozen cooking prawns, de-frosted and well drained
1 large courgette, sliced

15ml/1tbsp crème fraîche
30ml/2tbsp fresh coriander, chopped
salt and pepper
4 naan bread, warmed
150g/5oz natural yoghurt

Method

Heat the oil and gently fry the onions and garlic until soft.

Adding the tomato, curry paste and mango chutney. Simmer for 15 minutes.

Add the prawns, courgette, crème fraîche and 15ml/1tbsp of the coriander.

Season with sea salt and pepper and cook for a further 10 minutes.

Sprinkle with the remaining coriander and serve with naan bread and yoghurt.

Crab & Ginger Saffron Ravioli with a Lobster Bisque Sauce

Preparation Time: 10 to 30 minutes
Cooking Time: 1 to 2 hrs

Ingredients for 4
For the Ravioli:
200g/7oz fresh crab meat
2 shallots / 2 cloves garlic
15ml/1tbsp chopped ginger
1 stick lemongrass
30ml/2tbsp chopped coriander

3 eggs / 200g/7oz pasta flour
pinch of saffron dissolved in 30ml/2tbsp/1floz water
Sea Salt and Fresh Ground black pepper
Fresh chives

For the Lobster Bisque Sauce:
Lobster shells / Prawn shells
Splash of Brandy
30ml/2tbsp/1floz olive oil
_ Lemon / 1 Onion or 2 shallots
3 cloves Garlic
2 sticks Celery / 2 Carrots
6 Tomatoes
1 cup of Basmati or Long grain rice
5ml/1tsp Paprika
1 bay leaf
Sea Salt and Fresh Ground Black Pepper
2 glasses White Wine
50g/2oz Tomato puree
Double Cream / few knobs of unsalted Butter

Crab & Ginger Ravioli continued

Method

To prepare crab and ginger ravioli filling: Finely chop shallots, garlic, ginger, and lemongrass, and combine with crab meat. Add chopped coriander and seasoning to taste.
Add 1 egg combine and mix well.

To make pasta sheets: Combine flour, 2 eggs, saffron water, and pinch of salt. Form into a ball and knead dough for 10 minutes. Wrap with cling film and allow to rest in a refrigerator for at least 20 minutes. When ready to make pasta sheets, divide ball of dough into four, and roll out pasta sheets to thinnest setting in machine. Make ravioli in usual way.

To prepare lobster bisque sauce: Using a large saucepan, fry off lobster shells and prawn shells in a little olive oil for 5 minutes. Add a dash of brandy and flambé. Add chopped onion or shallots, garlic, celery and carrot, and fry for a further 5 minutes. Add chopped tomatoes, rice, paprika, bay leaf and seasoning, and stir well. Add lemon juice, white wine, tomato puree and water to cover. Bring to boil and then gently simmer for 1 hour, skimming the surface periodically to remove scum.

Pass through a fine-meshed sieve and return to saucepan and gently reduce to half the volume. Gently whisk in double cream and butter until sauce thickens, season to taste. (Alternatively, strain tin of Lobster Bisque Soup into a saucepan, and reduce. Add double cream, butter and seasoning as required).

Boil ravioli in salted water for few minutes until al dente. Drain and serve in shallow dish with lobster bisque sauce. Garnish with chopped chives.

Pan Fried Scallops with Sauce Vierge

Preparation and cooking time - under 30 minutes

Ingredients for 4

150ml / _ pint Olive oil
24 Scallops out of shell, coral removed
salt and pepper
5ml / 1tsp coriander seeds, lightly crushed
1 large tomato, skinned and diced
1 clove of garlic, peeled and crushed
Juice of 1 lemon

25g / 1oz fresh basil, shredded Fresh Basil to garnish

Method

Use a little of the oil to brush the scallops, then season them with sea salt and pepper. Heat a dry pan until very hot and sear the Scallops on each side for 1 minute. Arrange 6 scallops on each plate. Warm the remaining oil in a pan and add the coriander seeds, tomato and garlic. Stir in the lemon juice and basil, then spoon the oil over the Scallops. A few basil sprigs make an attractive garnish.

Sweet & Sour Sauce
This quick home-made recipe has health giving benefits as well as adding a wonderful flavour to a stir fry or meat dish. I have used this sauce many times to the pleasure of my guests. It is not suitable for diabetics due to the honey, but otherwise it can be used by the unwell. The sauce may be added to your recipe or served as a side dish.

Ingredients Serves 4
150ml Tomato pure or Tomato Sauce
75ml Local Honey
100ml Cider Vinegar (reduce by half if tomato sauce used)
A slate of flour for thickening

In a saucepan add all the ingredients and bring up to boiling, adjust thickness with slate of flour and taste by adjusting vinegar.

Sweet & Sour BBQ Sauce
Ideal for meat style dishes such barbequed chicken. This is superb as an addition or accompaniment with your BBQ.
Ingredients Serves 4 (multiply to serve more)

150ml Tomato Pure or tomato sauce
50ml light Soy sauce / 50ml Chilli bean sauce
75ml Hoisin sauce
2 large cloves Garlic
1 Tbsp fresh chopped Ginger
50ml Cider Vinegar / 75ml Local Honey
100ml Cider Vinegar / A slake of flour

Combine all ingredients in a blender for 5 seconds. Place in a pan and heat until hot.
Adjust thickness with slake of flour.
Adjust how hot you want it with Chilli Bean Sauce.
Anyone on restricted diet must ensure the ingredients are suitable

Chicken Casserole With Orange.
Ingredients Serves 4

1 _ Tbsp of Olive Oil
1kg of Skinless Chicken pieces (thigh is ideal)
1 Tbsp clove of Garlic – Finely chopped
1 Tbsp Fresh Root Ginger – finely chopped
Tbsp Black beans – drained (see tip below)
2 Tbsp Orange rind – shredded or grated
150ml Fresh squeezed Orange juice
2 Tbsp Chilli bean sauce

Small black soybeans are often bought in tins – drain and rinse thoroughly in clean water.

Heat the oil in a large flameproof casserole, quickly brown the chicken pieces on both sides. Remove chicken and add garlic, ginger, black beans, and orange rind and stir these for about 30 seconds making sure not to burn.

Add the rest of the sauces and ingredients and bring to the boil then simmer for 20 minutes or until chicken is cooked.

Test chicken with skewer to ensure juices run clear.

Serve hot with rice or noodles.

Chicken Biryani

This recipe is many hundreds of years old and from the area of Hyderabad. To get the best from this dish you must take care in the preparation and ingredients. Follow the recipe fully and this dish will delight any guest.

Preparation Time: 30 + 30 minutes
Cooking Time: 2 Hours
Ingredients for 4

1kg Fresh Boneless Chicken Breast and Thigh
2.5cm of Fresh Ginger   1 tsp Chilli Powder
6 cloves of Garlic   _ tsp Ground Turmeric
_ kg Basmati rice   900ml Water

Olive Oil for deep frying
4 Large Onions, finely sliced
4 green Chillies, deseeded and chopped
250ml Natural Yoghurt, beaten
250ml Milk
Handful each of Coriander and Mint leaves, chopped
The Juice of a Lemon
1 Tbsp of Concentrated Butter or Ghee
3 strands of Saffron soaked in 4 Tbsp hot milk
125ml Hot Water
Sea Salt to taste

Blend the ginger, garlic, chilli powder, ground turmeric and salt to a paste. Mix the paste well into the meat and stand to one side. In a Wok or large pan, heat the oil and fry the onions until they are a deep brown and crisp, but not burnt. Remove onions from oil with a slotted spoon to absorbent paper, reserving the oil. Reserve two Tbsp of onions for garnish, then crush the rest and add to paste with the chicken.

Put rice into saucepan of water and a little salt and bring to the boil, then drain off water and set aside.

Take a large heavy saucepan with tight fitting lid and add 4 Tbsp of the oil in which the onions were fried. Then evenly cover the base with chicken.

Mix the yoghurt, milk, half the Coriander and Mint leaves, all of the Chillies, Cardamom seeds and Lemon juice together. Sprinkle half of this mixture over the meat, then, spread evenly half of the rice over the meat. Sprinkle the rest of the Coriander and Mint over the layer of rice. Layer the rest of the rice and the meat and then pour over the rest of the second half of the yoghurt mixture. Make sure the last layer is of rice. Make deep holes into the dish with the handle of a wooden spoon and into each hole pour a little of the dissolved Saffron. Sprinkle the water over the top layer of rice and add a little concentrated butter or ghee

Cover the pan with a sheet of foil and then the lid. Weight the lid down if possible. Place on the lowest heat (use a heat diffuser if

heat is too high). Allow the Biryani to cook very slowly until the rice and the meat are cooked.
Check after 30 minutes by pinching a few grains of rice or putting a knife through the dish-it should come out clean. If it not ready and all the water has evaporated, sprinkle hot water and leave to cook again tightly covered. When checking dish work quickly as you do not want to loose too much steam.
Before serving gently mix the meat and rice and then garnish with the reserved onions

Serve with:
Egg Curry, Yoghurt with Cucumber and Mint

This dish may also be made with the same quantity of Lamb, Fish or Prawn

Organic Meat Suppliers

Berkshire: Sheppard's, 16 High Street, Goring on Thames, Reading, Berkshire, RG8 9AR. Tel: 01491 875142
Birmingham: Organic Roots, Crabtree Farm, Dark Lane, Kings Norton, B38 OBS. Tel: 01564 822294 / www.organicroots.co.uk
Cambridgeshire: The Horse and Gate Farm, Witcham Toll, Ely, Cambs, CB6 2AB Tel: 01353 778523
Devon: Higher Hacknell Farm, Burrington, Umberleigh, Devon, EX37 9LX. Tel: 01769 560909
Lloyd Maunder, Willand, Cullompton, Devon, EX15 2PJ
Tel: 01884 820534 / www.meatdirect.co.uk
Dorset: Heritage Prime, Shedbush Farm, Muddyfoot Lane, Stanton St. Gabriel, Bridport, Dorset, DT6 6OR
Tel: 01297 489304 / e-mail: heritageprime@aol.com

Heritage Prime produce also available from:
Holland Park, London. Tel: 020 7727 8243
Kentish Town, London. Tel: 020 7485 0346
Tamarisk Farm, West Bexington, Dorchester, Dorset, DT2 9DF
Tel: 01308 897781
East Sussex: Seasons, 10 Hartfield Row, Forest Row, E.Sussex, RH18 5DN. Tel: 01342 824673
Essex: The Happy Caterpillar, 92 Leigh Road, Leigh on Sea, SS9 1BU. Tel: 01702 712982
French's, Wigley Bush Lane, Brentwood, Essex
Herefordshire:
Natural Meats Direct, Model Farm, Hildersley, Ross-on-Wye, HR9 7NN. Tel: 01989 562208
Gloucestershire:
Colin J. Tyler, Down Barn, Trull Farm, Cherington Tetbury, Tel: 01285 841840 / e-mail: colin@downbarn.freeserve.co.uk
London:
W.J. Miller, 14 Stratford Road, Kensington, W8 6QD
Tel: 020 7937 1777
The Fresh Food Company, 326 Portobello Road, W10 5RU
Tel: 020 8969 0351 / www.freshfood.co.uk

Norfolk:
Elm House Farm, St Margarets, Harleston, Norfolk, IP20 OPJ
Tel: 01986 782421 / www.organics@hawkin.co.uk
Oxon: Eastbrook Farm Shop, Shrivenham, Oxon.
Tel: 01793 790460
Suffolk: Longwood Farm, Tuddenham St. Mary, Bury St. Edmunds, Suffolk, IP28 6TB. Tel: 01638 717120
Wiltshire: Rushall Farm Shop, Devizes Road, Rushall, Pewsey, Wilts, SN9 6ET. Tel: 01980 630335 / www.rushallorganics.co.uk
Worcestershire: Cridlaw and Walker, 23 Abbey Road, Gt Malvern, Worc WR14 3ET / Tel: 01684 573008
Scotland:
Damhead Organic Farm Shop, 32A Damhead,
Old Pentland Road, Lothianburn, Edinburgh, EH10 7EA.

Tel: 0131 445 1490
Jamesfield Farm, Jamesfield, Newburgh, Fife, KY14 6EW
Tel: 01738 850498 / www.jamesfieldfarm.co.uk
Lock Arthur Creamery, Beeswing, Dumfries, DG2 8JQ
Tel: 01387 760296

Therapeutic Recipes

Calcium Citrate:
(Pure organic). This is a pure organic form of calcium easily absorbed by the body. The ingredient MUST be organic and fresh. You will need 3 medium size eggs (fresh free range) 4 to 6 fresh Organic Lemons. Take the eggs wash the shells thoroughly and place in a glass bowl. Squeeze the juice from the lemons and cover eggs with the juice. Loosely cover the bowl and place in the refrigerator for about 48 hours until all the shell has been dissolved. The lemon juice will dissolve the outer shell (calcium) of the eggs and you will be left with whole eggs but in a soft sack. Remove eggs carefully and use for another dish. Take _ teaspoon of the lemon juice and calcium each day and no more otherwise

you may suffer cramp. I used this as part of my diet to restore calcium to my bones.

Kombucha:
Komucha is an effective metabolic balancer (helping the various organs work together), probiotic (supporting the beneficial bacteria), adaptogen (balancing the processes that get out of kilter) and detoxifier.

Lycopene:
The redness in tomatoes. An antioxidant. Found to be of benefit to sufferers of prostate cancer. The University of Illinois has positive findings from studies of women with cervix cancer.

Mucilage:
A gum like substance that is found in the plants seeds cell wall or seed case. This seed case cover is a polysaccharide which has a soothing effect on inflamed tissue. They are also used as an ingredient in some cosmetic preparations.

Sources

Coffee Mill/Grinder:
Kenwood Model CG100 costing about £17.00, available Powerhouse, John Lewis larger J. Sainsbury's stores or most good electrical stores.

Apple Cider Vinegar
Holland & Barrett – 'Honeygar' a mixture of honey and ACV. Lignan Nutrition 01708 741096

Borage oil:
Contact Lignan Nutrition on 01708 741096

Essentially Mine

Contact Lignan Nutrition 01708 741096

Flax seed oil, Whole seed and Flax seed flake:
Stone Mills Organic Oils
Mail Order - Telephone: 0800 093 1214

Fruit & Vegetable Juicers:
John Lewis Stores, Bentals, House of Fraser
And most good electrical stores.

Kombucha Tea:
The Kombucha Tea Network UK, PO Box 1887, Bath, BA2 8YA

Purple Grape Juice:
Welch's American Concorde: Sainsbury's, Tesco or Waitrose

Quark:
In my opinion Sainsbury's have the best quality although available from Tesco, Waitrose and other large stores.

Health Care Associations

AIDS Helpline 0800 567123
Alzheimer's Disease Society, Gordon House, 10 Greencoat Place, London, SW1 1PH. 020 7306 0606
Arthritic Association:
1 Little New Street, London, EC4A 3TR / Tel: 020 7491 0233
National Asthma Campaign
300 Upper Street, London N1 2XX / Tel (helpline): 0345 010203
National Back Pain Association
76 Elm Tree Road, Teddington, TW11 5ST / Tel: 020 8977 5474
Diabetics UK
10 Queen Anne Street, London, W1M 0BD / Tel: 020 7323 1531
Eating Disorders Association
Sackville Place, 44 Magdalen Street, Norwich, Norfolk, NR3 1JE

Tel: 01603 621414
National Eczema Society
163 Eversholt Street, London, NW1 1BU / Tel: 020 7388 4079
British Epilepsy Association, 40 Hanover Square,
Leeds LS3 1BE Tel: 01132 439393
British Kidney Patients Association, Tel: 01420 472021
ME Action, PO Box 1302, Wells, Somerset BA5 1YE
Tel: 01749 670799
Motor Neurone Disease, Box 246, Northampton, NN1 2PR
Tel: 01604 250505
MS Society, Tel: 020 77736 6267
Muscular Dystrophy, Tel: 020 7720 8055
Royal National Institute for the Blind, 224 Great Portland Street, London, W1N 6AA / Tel: 020 7388 1266
Chest, Heart and Stroke Association, CHSA House, Whitecross Street, London, EC1Y 8JJ / Tel: 020 7490 7999
Coelic Society, PO Box 220, High Wycombe, Bucks HP11 2HY
Tel: 01494 437278
British Colostomy Association
15 Station Road, Reading, Berkshire RG1 1LG
Tel: 0118 939 1537
Royal National Institute for the Deaf, 19-23 Featherstone Street, London, EC1Y 8SL / Tel: 020 7296 8000
The Ileostomy, Internal Pouch Support Group
PO Box 132, Scunthorpe, DN15 9YW. Tel: 01724 720150
Bowel Cancer
PO Box 360, Twickenham TW1 1UN Tel: 020 8892 5256
Colon Cancer Concern
4 Rickett Street, London SW6 1RU. Tel: 020 7381 4711

Cancer Organisations
Cancer Care Society
11 The Cornmarket, Romsey, Hampshire SO51 8GB
Tel: 01794 830300
Website: www.cancercaresoc.demon.co.uk
CancerLink

11-21 Northdown Street, London N1 9BN
Tel: (020) 7833 2818 Website: www.cancerlink.org
Macmillan Cancer Relief
89 Albert Embankment, London SE1 7UQ
Tel: 0845 601 601 (info line)
Marie Curie Cancer Care
28 Albert Embankment, London SE1 7TP
Tel: (020) 77599 7777
The Ulster Cancer Foundation
40-42 Eglanton Avenue, Belfast BT9 6DX
Tel: (028) 9066 3439 (helpline)

Distributed by AOI & Lignan Nutritional Publications
firexit@globalnet.co.uk
Tel: +44 (0)1708 741096